A Foreign Exchange Primer

For other titles in the Wiley Trading series
please see www.wiley.com/finance

A FOREIGN EXCHANGE PRIMER

Second Edition

Shani Shamah

WILEY

A John Wiley and Sons, Ltd., Publication

Published by   John Wiley & Sons Ltd, The Atrium, Southern Gate, Chichester,
                  West Sussex PO19 8SQ, England

                  Telephone   (+44) 1243 779777

Email (for orders and customer service enquiries): cs-books@wiley.co.uk
Visit our Home Page on www.wiley.com

Other Wiley Editorial Offices

John Wiley & Sons Inc., 111 River Street, Hoboken, NJ 07030, USA

Jossey-Bass, 989 Market Street, San Francisco, CA 94103-1741, USA

Wiley-VCH Verlag GmbH, Boschstr. 12, D-69469 Weinheim, Germany

John Wiley & Sons Australia Ltd, 42 McDougall Street, Milton, Queensland 4064, Australia

John Wiley & Sons (Asia) Pte Ltd, 2 Clementi Loop #02-01, Jin Xing Distripark, Singapore 129809

John Wiley & Sons Canada Ltd, 6045 Freemont Blvd, Mississauga, ONT, L5R 4J3, Canada

Library of Congress Cataloging-in-Publication Data

Shamah, Shani.
    A foreign exchange primer / Shani Shamah. — 2nd ed.
        p. cm.
    Includes bibliographical references and index.

    ISBN 978-0-470-75437-5

    1. Foreign exchange futures.   2. Foreign exchange market.   I. Title.
    HG3853.S53 2008
    332.4'5—dc22   2008040294

Typeset in 10/12pt Times by Aptara Inc., New Delhi, India
Printed and bound in Great Britain by TJ International Ltd, Padstow, Cornwall, UK

Contents

Disclaimer

This publication is for information purposes only and contains advice, recommendations and/or opinions that may be used as the basis for trading.

The publication should not be construed as solicitation or as offering advice for the purposes of the purchase or sale of any financial product. The information and opinions contained within this publication were considered to be valid when published.

The charts, additional examples and pictures have been kindly supplied by MMS, 4castweb.com and GFT Global Markets.

While MMS, 4CAST Limited and GFT Global Markets have attempted to be as accurate as possible with the information presented here, they do not guarantee its accuracy or completeness and make no warranties of merchantability or fitness for a particular purpose. In no event shall they be liable for direct, indirect or incidental, special or consequential damages resulting from the information herein regardless of whether such damages were foreseen or unforeseen. Any opinions expressed in this publication are given in good faith, but are subject to change without notice.

Please note: All rates and figures used in the examples are for illustrative purposes only. The contents are copyright Shani Shamah 2008 and should not be used or distributed without the author's prior agreement.

1
Introduction

1.1 THE FOREIGN EXCHANGE MARKET

The foreign exchange market is by far the largest financial market in the world and thrives on its enormous ocean of money. It trades across the world with an estimated $ 3.2 trillion* global average daily volume, which solidifies foreign exchange as an asset class. It is distinguished from other markets, for example the commodity or equity markets, by having no fixed base – no centralized marketplace. In other words, the foreign exchange market exists at the end of a telephone, the Internet or other means of instant communication; it is not located in a building, nor is it limited by fixed trading hours. Hence, unlike equities, foreign exchange has not traditionally traded in one single location, such as on a regulated exchange, but it has always been a disjointed market where trading primarily takes place in an over-the-counter market where buyers and sellers conduct business. The foreign exchange market is truly a 24-hour global trading system where traders of all types and sizes can participate. It knows no barriers and trading activity in general moves with the sun from one major financial centre to the next, starting with Wellington and Sydney and moving through the time zones and trading centres of Tokyo, Hong Kong, Singapore, London and New York to the West Coast of America. Anything that happens anywhere in the world, no matter at what time of the day or night, like terrorist attacks, US sub-prime market woes, geopolitical tensions over nuclear power, oil supply problems and pricing, and many other issues which can threaten to disrupt trade and economic relationships, will affect the foreign exchange market instantly. Reports and events reported in Japan will have an effect on happenings in all foreign exchange trading centres across the globe, thus making foreign exchange a truly global trading asset.

---

* *BIS Triennial Central Bank Survey of FX and Derivatives Market Activity in April 2007, published September and December 2007*

> The foreign exchange market is a global network of buyers and sellers of currencies.
>
> Foreign exchange or FX or Forex comprises all claims to foreign currency payable abroad, whether consisting of funds held in foreign currency with banks abroad, or bills or cheques payable abroad; i.e. it is the exchange of one currency for another.
>
> A foreign exchange transaction is a contract to exchange one currency for another currency at an agreed rate on an agreed date.

1.2   VALUE TERMS

Throughout history, one person has traded with another, sometimes to obtain desired raw materials by barter, sometimes to sell finished products for money, and sometimes to buy and sell commodities or goods for no other reason than to make a profit from the transactions involved. The pre-historic 'bartering' of goods and the use of cowrie shells or similar objects of value as payment eventually gave way, approximately 4000 years ago, to the use of coins struck in precious metals. Even in those far-off days, there was international trade and payments were settled in any coinage that was acceptable to both parties. Early Greek coins, which were almost universally accepted in the then known world, were soon given values in terms of their models, and a price for any raw material or finished goods could be quoted in value terms of either Greek originals or other nations' copies.

The first forward foreign exchange transactions can be traced back to the money-changers in Lombardy in the 1500s. Foreign exchange, as we know it today, has its roots in the Gold Standard, which was introduced in 1880. It was a system of fixed exchange rates in relation to gold and the absence of any exchange controls.

1.3   COFFEE HOUSES

Banking and financial markets closer to those of today were started in the coffee houses of European financial centres, such as the City of London. In the seventeenth century these coffee houses became the meeting places not only of merchants seeking to trade their finished goods, but also of those who bought and sold solely for profit. It is the City of London's domination of these early markets that saw it maturing through the powerful late Victorian era, and it was strong enough to survive two world wars and the depression of the 1930s.

1.4   SPOT AND FORWARD MARKET

Today, foreign exchange is an integral part of our daily lives. Without foreign exchange, international trade would not be possible. For example, a Swiss watchmaker will incur expenses in Swiss francs. When the company wants to sell the watches, they want to receive Swiss francs to meet those expenses. However, if they sell to an English merchant, the English company will want to pay in sterling, the home currency. In between, a transaction has to occur that converts one currency into the other. That transaction is undertaken in the foreign exchange market. However, foreign exchange does not only involve trade. Trade, today, is only a small part of the foreign exchange market; movements of international capital seeking the most profitable home for the shortest term dominates.

The main participants in the foreign exchange market are:

- Commercial banks – participate in the markets from the point of view of managing their own foreign exchange risks and that of their clients, and should they have a particularly strong view will also speculate on currency movements.
- Commercial organisations – by the nature of their business, companies could engage in commercial or capital transactions that require them to enter the currency markets to either buy or sell foreign currencies.
- Brokers – acts as a middleman in the same way as a stockbroker in the equities market, but brokers confine their activities to acting between banks and do not accept orders from corporate or retail clients.
- Central banks – their role tends to be diverse and can differ from country to country, however most are charged with the responsibility of maintaining an orderly market for the national currency.
- Fund managers – tend to invest across a range of countries and investment asset classes on behalf of their clients, for instance pension funds and individual investors.
- Hedge funds – have a tendency to be very aggressive in their investment approach and are generally concerned with managing the total risk of a pooled investment.
- Speculators – in the narrow sense of the financial markets, buy, hold and sell (and vice versa) to profit from fluctuations in foreign exchange prices.
- Retail traders and investors – a new breed of participant into the foreign exchange market and have the same goals as everyone else – to make money.

Most participants transact in foreign currency, not only for immediate delivery but also for settlement at specific times in the future. By using the forward markets, the participant can

---

A spot transaction is where delivery of the currencies is two business days from the trade date (except the Canadian dollar, which is one day).

A forward transaction is any transaction that settles on a date beyond spot.

determine today the currency equivalent of future foreign currency flows by trans-
ferring the risk of currency fluctuations (hedging or covering foreign currency
exposure). The market participants on the other side of any trade must either have
exactly opposite hedging needs or be willing to take a speculative position. The most
common method used by participants when transacting in either spot or forward
foreign currency is to deal directly with a bank, although Internet trading is currently
making impressive inroads.

These banks usually have large foreign exchange sales and trading departments that
not only handle the requests from their clients but also take positions to make trading
profits and balance foreign currency positions arising from other bank business.
Typical transactions in the bank market range from $1 million to $500 million,
although banks will handle smaller amounts as requested by their clients at slightly
less favourable terms.

1.5   ALTERNATIVE MARKETS

In addition to the spot and forward markets, other markets have been developed that
are gaining acceptance. Foreign currency future contracts provide an alternative to
the forward market and have been designed for dealing with major currencies. These
contracts have the advantages of

> **A currency future obligates its owner to purchase a specified asset at a speci-
> fied exercise price on the contract maturity date.**

smaller contract sizes and a high degree of liquidity for small transactions. The
disadvantages include the inflexibility of standardized contract sizes, maturities, and
higher costs on large transactions. Options on both currency futures and on spot
currency are also available. Another

> **An option gives the owner the right but not the obligation to buy or sell a
> specified quantity of a currency at a specified rate on or before a specified
> date.**

technique that is used to provide long-dated forward cover of foreign currency exposure, especially against the currency flow of foreign currency debt, is a foreign
currency swap.

> **A foreign currency swap is where two currencies are exchanged for an agreed
> period of time and re-exchanged at maturity at the same exchange rate.**

CONCLUDING REMARKS

In summary, the foreign exchange market is open for business 24-hours a day (almost seven days a week but not quite) with liquidity not being a major problem in most locations. In addition, with the advances in technology, trading over electronic platforms is becoming the norm, where foreign exchange trades are executed instantaneously. Plus, the foreign exchange market provides some of the highest leverage of any investment instrument, where it is possible to trade a sizeable position with limited funds via margin trading. It is a market which will take into account gut feelings, fundamental, economic and technical factors with enough volatility to satisfy the majority. Simply put, foreign exchange is an efficient market whereby the rates quoted by any market participant reflects all news, supply and demand issues, which way the market is weighted and potentially resting orders.

Perhaps most importantly, the foreign exchange market has depth and breadth superior to any capital markets instrument. For instance, equities, whether cash or derivatives, are all subject to what is available in an 'order book' and orders of any size may have to be worked before being filled. On the other hand, a foreign exchange order could be filled at one rate in a reasonable size instantaneously.

Although activity in the foreign exchange market remains predominately the domain of the large professional players – for example, major international banks, such as Citigroup, JPMorgan, HSBC and Deutsche Bank, it does not mean that the market is totally dominated by or controlled by such institutions. Other players also live in this market and include amongst others corporations, fund managers, brokers, speculators and retail investors. Though a bank's scale of trading is vast compared to the average retail trader, they are all concerned by and affected by the same issues and happenings of the day. When all said and done, all participants, whether large or small, seek to make a profit out of their activities in the foreign exchange market. However, with liquidity and the advent of Internet trading, plus the availability of margin trading, this 24-hour market requires a much disciplined approach to trading, as profit opportunities and potential loss are equal and opposite.

Part I
Market Overview

2
A Brief History of the Market

Foreign exchange is the medium through which international debt is both valued and settled. It is also a means of evaluating one country's worth in terms of another's and, depending on circumstances, can therefore exist as a store of value.

> **Between 9000 and 6000 BC cattle (cows, sheep, camels) were used as the first and oldest form of money.**

2.1 THE BARTER SYSTEM

Throughout history, people have traded for various reasons: sometimes to obtain desired raw materials by barter; sometimes to sell finished products for money; and sometimes to buy and sell commodities or other goods for no other reason than to try to profit from the transaction involved. For example, a farmer might need grain to make bread while another farmer might have a need for meat. They would, therefore, have the opportunity to agree terms, whereby one farmer could exchange his grain for the cow on offer from the other farmer. The barter system, in fact, provided a means for people to obtain the goods they needed as long as they had goods or services that were required by other people.

This system worked quite well and, even today, barter, as a system of exchange, remains in use throughout the world and sometimes in quite a sophisticated way. For example, during the cold war when the Russian rouble was not an exchangeable currency, the only way that Russia could obtain a much-needed commodity, such as wheat, was to arrange to obtain it from another country in exchange for a different commodity. Due to bad harvests in Russia, wheat was in short supply, while America had a surplus. America also had a shortage of oil, which was in excess in Russia. Thus Russia delivered oil to America in exchange for wheat.

Although the barter system worked quite well, it was not perfect. For instance it lacked:

- *Convertibility* – What is the value of a cow? In other words, what could a cow convert into?
- *Portability* – How easy is it to carry a cow around?
- *Divisibility* – If a cow is deemed to be worth three pigs, how much of a cow would one pig be worth?

It was the introduction of paper money – which had the three characteristics lacking in the barter system – that allowed the development of international commerce as we know it today.

2.2   THE INTRODUCTION OF COINAGE

Approximately 4000 years ago, pre-historic bartering of goods or similar objects of value as payment eventually gave way to the use of coins struck in precious metals. An important concept of early money was that it was fully backed by a reserve of gold and was convertible to gold (or silver) at the holder's request.

Even in those days, there was international trade and payments were settled in such coinage as was acceptable to both parties. Early Greek coins were almost universally accepted in the then known world; in fact, many Athenian designs were frequently mimicked, proving the coinage's popularity in design as well as acceptability.

Cowries (shells) were viewed as money in 1200 BC.

The first metal money and coins appeared in China in 1000 BC. The coins were made of base metals, often containing holes so that they could be put together like a chain.

The first paper bank notes appeared in China in 800 AD and, as a result, currency exchange started between some countries.

2.3   THE EXPANDING BRITISH EMPIRE

Skipping through time, some banking and financial markets nearer to those we know today began in the coffee houses of European financial centres. In the seventeenth century these coffee houses became the meeting places of merchants wishing to trade their finished products and of the entrepreneurs of the day. Soon after the Battle of Waterloo, during the nineteenth century, foreign trade from the expanding British Empire – and the finance required to fuel the industrial revolution – increased the size and frequency of international monetary transfers. For various reasons, a substitute for the large-scale transfer of coins or bullion had to be found (the 'Dick Turpin' era) and the bill of exchange for commercial purposes and its personal account equivalent, the cheque, were both born. At this time, London was building itself a reputation as the world's capital for trade and finance, and the City became a natural centre for the negotiation of all such instruments, including foreign-drawn bills of exchange.

2.4   THE GOLD STANDARD

> **Gold was officially made the standard value in England in the nineteenth century. The value of paper money was tied directly to gold reserves in America.**

Foreign exchange, as we know it today, has its roots in the Gold Standard, which was introduced in 1880. The main features were a system of fixed exchange rates in relation to gold and the absence of any exchange controls. Under the Gold Standard, a country with a balance of payments deficit had to surrender gold, thus reducing the volume of currency in the country, leading to deflation. The opposite occurred to a country with a balance of payments surplus.

Thus the Gold Standard ensured the soundness of each country's paper money and, ultimately, controlled inflation as well. For example, when holders of paper money in America found the value of their dollar holdings falling in terms of gold, they could exchange dollars for gold. This had the effect of reducing the amount of dollars in circulation. Inevitably, as the supply of dollars fell, its value stabilized and then rose. Thus, the exchange of dollars for gold reserves was reversed. As long as the discipline of linking each currency's value to the value of gold was maintained, the simple laws of supply and demand would dictate both currency valuation and the economics of the country.

The Gold Standard of exchange sounded ideal:

- inflation was low;
- currency values were linked to a universally recognized store of value;
- interest rates were low, meaning that inflation was virtually nonexistent.

The Gold Standard survived until the outbreak of World War I, after which foreign exchange, as we know it today, really began. Currencies were convertible into either gold or silver, but the main currencies for trading purposes were the British pound and, to a lesser extent, the American dollar. The amounts were relatively small by today's transactions, and the trading centres tended to exist in isolation.

> **The early twentieth century saw the end of the Gold Standard.**

2.5   THE BRETTON WOODS SYSTEM

Convertibility ended with the Great Depression, and the major powers left the Gold Standard and fostered protectionism. As the political climate deteriorated and the world headed for war, the foreign exchange markets all but ceased to exist. With the end of World War II, reconstruction for Europe and the Far East had as its base the Bretton Woods system.

In 1944 the Bretton Woods agreement devised a system of convertible currencies, fixed rates and free trade.

In 1944, the post-war system of international monetary exchange was established at Bretton Woods in New Hampshire, USA. The intent was to create a gold-based value of the American dollar and the British pound and link other major currencies to the dollar. This system allowed for small fluctuations in a 1 % band.

2.6   THE INTERNATIONAL MONETARY FUND AND THE WORLD BANK

The conference, in fact, rejected a suggestion by Keynes for a new world reserve currency in favour of a system built on the dollar. To help to accomplish its objectives, the Bretton Woods conference instigated the creation of the International Monetary Fund (IMF) and the World Bank. The function of the IMF was to lend foreign currency to members who required assistance, funded by each member according to size and resources. Gold was pegged at $ 35 an ounce. Other currencies were pegged to the dollar and under this system, inflation would be precluded among the member nations.

In the years following the Bretton Woods agreement, recovery was soon evident, trade expanded and foreign exchange dealings, while primitive by today's standards, returned. While the amount of gold held in the American central reserves remained constant, the supply of dollar currency grew. In fact, the increased supply of dollars in Europe funded the post-war reconstruction of Europe in the 1950s. It seemed that the Bretton Woods accord had achieved its purpose. However, events in the 1960s once again brought turmoil to the currency markets and threatened to unravel the agreement.

2.7   THE DOLLAR RULES OK

By 1960, the dollar was supreme and the American economy was thought to be immune to adverse international developments, and the growing balance of payments deficits in America did not appear to alarm the authorities. The first cracks started to appear in November 1967. The British pound was devalued as a result of high inflation, low productivity and a worsening balance of payments. Not even massive selling by the Bank of England could avert the inevitable. President Johnson was trying to finance 'the great society' and fight the Vietnam War at the same time. This caused a drain on the gold reserves and led to capital controls.

In 1967, succumbing to the pressure of the diverging economic policies of the members of the IMF, Britain devalued the pound from $ 2.80 to $ 2.40. This not only increased demand for the dollar but it also increased the pressure on the dollar price of gold, which remained at $ 35 an ounce. Under this system free market forces were unable to find an equilibrium value.

2.8   SPECIAL DRAWING RIGHTS

By now markets were becoming increasingly unstable, reflecting confused economic and political concerns. In May 1968, France underwent severe civil disorder and had some of the worst street rioting in recent history. In 1969, France unilaterally devalued the franc and Germany was obliged to revalue the Deutschemark, resulting in a two-tier system of gold convertibility. Central banks agreed to trade gold at $ 35 an ounce with each other and not intercede in the open marketplace where normal pressures of supply and demand would dictate the prices.

> In 1968 the IMF created Special Drawing Rights (SDRs), which made international foreign exchange possible.
>
> In 1969, SDRs were approved as a form of reserve that central banks could exchange as a surrogate for gold.

As an artificial asset kept on the books of the IMF, SDRs were to be used as a surrogate for real gold reserves. Although the word 'asset' was not used, it was in fact an attempt by the IMF to create an additional form of paper gold to be traded between central banks. Later, the SDR was defined as a basket of currencies, although the composition of that basket has been changed several times since then.

> During 1971 the Bretton Woods agreement was dissolved.

2.9   A DOLLAR PROBLEM

As the American balance of payments worsened, money continued to flow into Germany. In April 1971, the German Central Bank intervened to buy dollars and sell Deutschemarks to support the flagging dollar. In the following weeks, despite massive action, market forces overwhelmed the central bank and the Deutschemark was allowed to revalue upwards against the dollar. In May 1971, Germany revalued again and other currencies quickly followed. The collapse of the Bretton Woods system finally occurred when the American authorities acknowledged that there was a 'dollar' problem. President Nixon closed 'the gold window' on 15 August 1971, thereby ending dollar convertibility into gold. He also declared a tax on all imports for a short period, but signalled to the market that a devaluation of the dollar versus the major European currencies and the Japanese yen was due.

2.9.1   The Smithsonian Agreement

A final attempt was made to repair the Bretton Woods agreement during late 1971 at a meeting at the Smithsonian Institute. The result was aptly known as the Smithsonian agreement. A widening of the official intervention bands for currency values of the Bretton Woods agreement from 1 % to 2.25 % was imposed, as well as a realignment of values and an increase in the official price of gold to $ 38 per ounce.

2.9.2   The Snake

With the Smithsonian agreement the dollar was devalued. Despite the fanfare surrounding the new agreement, Germany nevertheless acted to impose its own controls to keep the Deutschemark down. In concert with its Common Market colleagues, Germany fostered the creation of the first European Monetary system, known as the 'snake'. This system referred to the narrow fluctuation of the EEC currencies bound by the wider band of the non-EEC currencies. This short-lived system began in April 1972, but even this mechanism was not the panacea all had hoped for, and Britain left the snake, having spent millions in support of the pound.

2.9.3   The Dirty Float

During this period the dollar was still under pressure as money flowed into Germany, the rest of Europe and Japan. The final straw was the imposition of restrictions by the Italian government to support the Italian lira. This ultimately caused the demise of the Smithsonian agreement and led to a 10 % devaluation of the dollar in February 1973. Currencies now floated freely, with occasional central bank intervention. This was the era of the 'dirty float', and 1973 and 1974 saw a change in the dollar's fortunes. The four-fold increase in oil prices following the Yom Kippur War, in the Middle East, created a tremendous demand for dollars, and, since oil was priced in dollars the currency soared. Those who were accustomed to selling dollars were severely tried. The collapse of the Herstatt and Franklin banks followed as a direct result of this shift in the dollar's fortunes. The dollar was again under pressure during the mid-1970s, reflecting still worsening balance of payments figures. Treasury secretary Michael Blumenthal, in trying to foster export growth, constantly talked the dollar down, and Europe and Japan were glad to see a lower dollar, since their oil payments were correspondingly cheaper.

2.10   THE EMS AND THE ERM

The European Monetary System (EMS) and the European Rate Mechanism (ERM) were established in 1979.

2.10.1   The European Monetary System

In the EMS, member currencies were permitted to move within broad limits against each other and a central point. The EMS represented a further attempt at European economic coordination, and a grid was established, linking the value of each currency to the others. This attempt to 'fix' exchange rates met with near extinction during 1992–1993, when built-up economic pressures forced the devaluations of a number of weak European currencies.

The maximum permitted divergence from the EEC band of currency fluctuations was:

- 2.25 % among strong currencies within the EEC;
- 6.00 % among weak currencies within the EEC;
- Unlimited with other countries and the dollar.

Divergence beyond these boundaries required the central banks of each country to intervene in the foreign exchange markets, selling the strong currency and buying the weak to maintain their relative values.

2.10.2   The Exchange Rate Mechanism

In 1979, central banks agreed to another tool to intervene in the market. This was known as the Exchange Rate Mechanism (ERM), and allowed changes in short-term interest rates thus punishing speculators by raising rates in the weaker currencies to discourage short selling. Currencies participating in the ERM were:

- Austrian schilling;
- Belgium franc;
- Danish krone;

- German Mark;
- French franc;
- Portuguese escudo;
- Spanish peseta;
- Dutch guilder;
- Irish punt.

2.11   THE EUROPEAN CURRENCY UNIT

The European Currency Unit (ECU) was also introduced as a forerunner to creating a single European currency. The ECU was a currency based on the weighted average of the currencies of the common market. The ECU also served to provide a measure of relative value for each currency in the EMS.

An active market in ECU-denominated bonds developed, as well as a liquid spot and forward ECU foreign exchange market. The primary activity in these markets was to supply liquidity through speculative trading and arbitrage of the component elements of the ECU. All such trading activity served to stabilize the currency and interest markets and was, therefore, valuable.

Throughout the 1980s, the EMS suffered occasional periods of stress in the system, with speculative runs on the weak currencies of the system resulting in frequent realignments. The German Bundesbank's conservative anti-inflationary policies were out of step with the more inflation-prone, loose money policies of Italy, France, Spain, Portugal and the Scandinavian countries. Devaluation of those currencies versus the Deutschemark was often associated with large speculative positions, which were taken by banks, hedge funds and other market participants, almost always at the expense of currency holders of the weaker countries.

2.12   THE MAASTRICHT TREATY

The quest for currency stability in Europe continued with the signing of the Maastricht treaty in 1991. This treaty proposed that a single European Central Bank be established, much as the Federal Reserve that was established in 1913 to act on behalf of American interests. After the European currencies were fixed, they were moved into a single currency, which has led to the actual replacement of many European currencies with the euro.

2.13   THE TREATY OF ROME

The euro has actually been an ambition since 1958 and the Treaty of Rome, with a declaration of a common European market as a European objective with the aim of increasing economic prosperity and contributing to 'an ever closer union among the people of Europe'. The Single European Act and the Treaty on European Union have built on this, introducing Economic and Monetary Union (EMU) and laying the foundations for a single currency.

In 1991 the European Council approved the Treaty of the European Union. Fifteen countries signed for the European currency – the euro.

In 1992, the EMS came under the most intense pressure in its short history. In September, Britain was forced out of the ERM after less than two years as a member. Germany's tight monetary policy proved incompatible with most of the other members of the EMS, leading to devaluations or total departures from the system.

From the summer of 1992 to 1993, speculators proved many times that the market in foreign exchange was far more potent a force in driving exchange rates than central banks. One of the most famous examples of speculation driving economic policy occurred when George Soros was reputed to have earned $1 billion selling British pounds and buying dollars and Deutschemarks by 'betting' against the ability of the central banks to withstand market forces.

In August 1993, the ERM intervention points were widened to 15% for most currencies – an admission by the central banks to the markets of their inability to dictate exchange rates. Speculators made fortunes in foreign exchange trading, betting against the central banks' capacity to manage foreign exchange rates in contradiction of the divergent economies and policies of the EMS members.

Periods of volatility are always associated with speculation, as the market attempts to find an equilibrium value for each currency that reflects all of the information in the marketplace. It is, in fact, the speculators that provide most of the capital in efforts to revalue or devalue a currency, rather than central banks' current reserves. For example, when the dollar reached its all-time low against the yen in 1995, the resulting loss of competitiveness of Japanese products globally caused a severe recession in Japan, leading to several bank failures, a real estate sell off globally, and drastic changes in economic and interest rate policies.

2.14   ECONOMIC REFORM

Similarly, in early 1998 the strength in the yen against all the major currencies was associated with high volatility and much speculative activity. The marketplace reacted to the political pressure imposed by America in attempting to reduce the trade imbalance between America and Japan by strengthening the yen. With the American Federal Reserve Bank intervening in the foreign exchange market to sell dollars and buy yen (Figure 2.1), coupled with threats of a trade war and import tariffs, the yen was significantly revalued upwards. However, in the second half of 1998, the financial

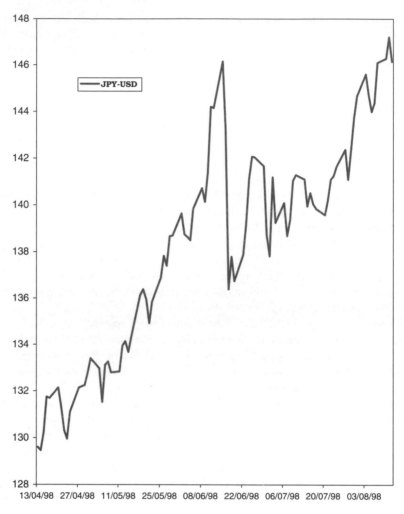

Figure 2.1 US Federal intervention on the dollar in 1998. Reproduced by permission of Standard & Poor's. *Source:* MMS

crisis in Asia, coupled with the opinion that the yen was severely overvalued, caused the yen to tumble against the dollar and other major currencies. Speculation in the marketplace, once again, had caused economic reform.

2.15 A COMMON MONETARY POLICY

The next stage of EMU began on 1 January 1999, when the exchange rates of the participating currencies were irrevocably set. Euro area member states began implementing a common monetary policy and the euro was introduced as legal tender. The 11 currencies of the participating member states became subdivisions of the euro with Greece becoming the twelfth member on 1 January 2001.

The composition of the European Central Bank occurred in 1998. Eleven countries sign for the euro: Austria, Belgium, Finland, France, Germany, Ireland, Italy, Luxembourg, Netherlands, Portugal and Spain. January 1999 was the conversion weekend. The equity markets of 11 European nations have been united into one monetary unit – the euro.

On 1 January 2001, Greece became the twelfth country to join the European Union.

2.16   THE SINGLE CURRENCY

In January 2002 the euro currency became the legal tender in all 12 participating countries.

In January 2002, euro notes and coins were actually being circulated in the different countries and by the end of the first quarter, national notes and coins no longer existed. This change had an impact on everyone, from manufacturers, importers and exporters with trade flows to hedge, central banks with reserve asset and debt management concerns, to financial institutions and pension funds with international portfolios. In fact, even though this event was specific to Europe, the impact affected the world's currency markets from America to Japan. The single currency in Europe formed one corner of the new triangular world of the dollar, the yen, and the euro.

However, the euro is not the currency of all EU Member States, even though all EMU members are eligible to adopt the euro. Denmark and the United Kingdom have opted to remain outside the euro for the time being, while Bulgaria, the Czech Republic, Estonia, Hungary, Latvia, Lithuania, Poland, Romania, and Sweden have no target date for joining.

The entry criteria for the euro includes two years of prior exchange rate stability via membership of the Exchange Rate Mechanism (ERM), which EU countries can join in order to keep their currency stable against the euro whether they intend eventually to adopt the single currency or not. Apart from exchange rate stability, there are four other criteria for adopting the euro. These relate to interest rates, the budget deficit, the inflation rate and the debt-to-GDP ratio.

The conversion of national legacy currencies meant that organizations had to have the ability to accept both forms of transaction. It has been quite complicated because, for instance, to convert sterling to francs you had to have a conversion via the euro. This is because the national legacy currency no longer existed in its own right but was a denomination of the euro, fixed by the conversion rate. These legacy rates are shown in Table 2.1.

Table 2.1   The fixing rates: legacy currencies rates against the euro

Austrian schilling	ATS	13.7603
Belgian franc	BEF	40.3399
Finnish mark	FIM	5.94573
French franc	FRF	6.55957
German Mark	DEM	1.95583
Greek drachma	GRD	340.75
Irish punt	IEP	0.787564
Italian lira	ITL	1936.27
Luxembourg franc	LUF	40.3399
Dutch guilder	NLG	2.20371
Portuguese escudo	PTE	200.482
Spanish peseta	ESP	166.386

The European currencies have always fluctuated against the dollar, even as the debate about the euro has raged, and this can be shown in the following.

- *Birth of European Monetary System.* The economic crisis of the 1970s led to the first plans for a single currency, and the system of fixed exchange rates pegged to the dollar was abandoned. European leaders agreed to create a 'currency snake', tying European currencies together. However, the system immediately came under pressure from the dollar, causing problems for some of the weaker European currencies.
- *Plaza Accord.* During the 1980s, the dollar-strengthened dramatically. American interest rates were high, which was caused by a dispute between the Reagan administration and the American Federal Reserve Bank over the size of the budget deficit. In 1986, the world's leading industrial countries agreed to act and lower the value of the dollar. A successful deal was struck at New York's Plaza hotel.
- *Kuwait crisis.* On 2 August 1990 Iraq invaded Kuwait. On the same day the UN Security Council passed a resolution condemning the invasion. The position of the Swiss franc against the dollar during 1990/1991 is shown in Figure 2.2.
- *Maastricht treaty.* In 1991, the 15 members of the European Union, meeting in the Dutch town of Maastricht, agreed to set up a single currency as part of a drive towards economic and monetary union. There were strict criteria for joining, including targets for inflation, interest rates and budget deficits. A European central bank was established to set interest rates. Britain and Denmark, however, opted out of these plans.
- *ERM crisis.* The exchange rate mechanism, established in 1979, was used to keep the value of European currencies stable. However, fears that voters might reject the Maastricht treaty led currency speculators to target the weaker currencies. In September 1992, Britain and a few of the other EU countries were forced to devalue, and only the French franc was successfully defended against the speculators.

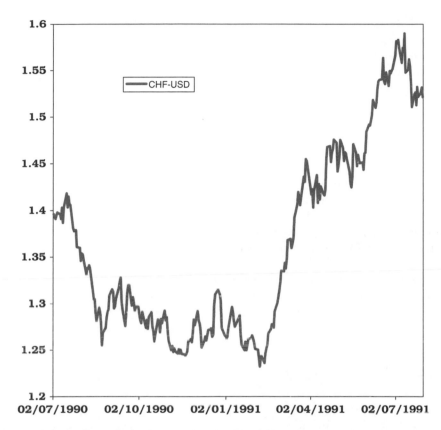

Figure 2.2   Dollar vs Swiss franc during the Kuwaiti invasion. Reproduced by permission of Standard & Poor's. *Source:* MMS

- *Asian crisis*. The turbulence in the Asian currency markets began in July 1997 in Thailand and quickly spread throughout the Asian economies, eventually reaching Russia and Brazil. Foreign lenders withdrew their funds amid fears of a global financial meltdown and the dollar strengthened. Many EU countries were struggling to cut their budget deficits to meet the criteria for euro membership.
- *Euro launch*. The euro was launched on 1 January 1999 as an electronic currency used by banks, foreign exchange dealers and stock markets. The new European Central Bank set interest rates across the eurozone. However, uncertainty about its policy and public disagreements among member governments weakened the value of the euro on the foreign exchange markets.
- *Central bank intervention*. After just 20 months, the euro had lost nearly 30 % in value against the dollar. The European Central Bank and other central banks finally joined forces to boost its value. This move helped to put a floor under the euro,

but it did not recover its value. A weak euro helped European exports, but it also undermined the credibility of the currency and fuelled inflationary pressures.

- *Terrorist attacks on New York and Washington*. The attack in New York severely tested the currency markets. Money flowed out of the dollar into safe havens, such as the Swiss franc and, for the first time, the euro. The central banks tried to calm the markets and interest rates were cut across the globe. Many observers believe it may have marked the coming of age of the euro as an international currency.
- *Euro became cash currency*. On 1 January 2002, the euro became a reality for approximately 300 million citizens of the 12 countries in the Eurozone. The arrival of the euro as a cash currency may foster closer integration and greater price competition within the Eurozone. It may, also, help to boost its international role, as the doubts grow over the strength of the dollar, especially as the American economy continues to slow.
- *Slovenia adopted the euro*. January 2007 after passing the test in 2006 to become the thirteenth EU country to use the euro – the first of the 2004 intake of members to do so.
- *Cyprus and Malta adopt the euro*. On 1 Janaury 2008 the Mediterranean holiday is-lands of Cyprus and Malta adopted the euro. These two islands, both former British colonies, scrapped the Cyprus pound (at the irrevocably fixed exchange rate of € 1 = CYP 0.585274) and Maltese lira (at the irrevocably fixed exchange rate of € 1 = MTL 0.429300), bringing the number of countries using the single currency to 15.
- *The future*. Slovakia plans to adopt the euro on 1 January 2009.

CONCLUDING REMARKS

Over the past 30 years or so, nations in the West have variously experienced currency devaluations, revaluations, the abandonment of the dollar – gold convertibility, oil crises, crises of confidence, exchange controls, snakes in tunnels, basket currencies, recycling pressure and the subsequent Third World debtor nations' crisis.

Commercial banks have historically been the conduit for international trade settle-ments, many of them playing a pivotal role in providing an indispensable service acting as the trustee in international trade, putting them squarely in the middle of the 'new' foreign exchange market. The banks recognized the signs early on and by the end of 1971, had already devoted substantial resources to this new and emerging market. International trade dominated flows in currencies in the initial years and international investing was still novel, expensive and different. Many developed countries, especially in Europe, maintained strict exchange and capital flow controls. Once banks realized that good money could be made in the foreign exchange market, newcomers started to crowd in. The result was an excess of market-maker banks, whose number peaked sometime in the mid 1980's.

Former British Prime Minister Margaret Thatcher was largely credited with firing the starting pistol to breaking down the barriers to international capital flows, another indication of the defunct Bretton Woods system. As the obstacles to cross-border investing began to disappear, and modern portfolio theory mandated more diversification, money managers started to look beyond their own borders for more opportunities to spread investment risk. International capital flows began to swell and soon dwarfed trade flows. The fact that the last great equity bear market of the twentieth century ended during 1974 also helped prepare the ground for the huge growth of the foreign exchange market. Much of the growth in investment activity was fuelled by the rapid expansion of government mandated private pension schemes, especially in Europe. Investment bankers began to appear on the foreign exchange market scene in order to cater to their clients' appetite for foreign investments.

However, on the whole, we now live in a world of freely floating exchange rates. There is a far better understanding of monetary economics on the part of the world's governments, much reduced dependence on artificial trade barriers or exchange controls and a freedom and speed of international communication, which creates a single global foreign exchange market.

It will be difficult to predict how the foreign exchange markets will perform in the next few years, but two points are certain:

- London will remain the largest foreign exchange centre, outperforming New York and Tokyo in volume.
- Risk management will continue to be a key issue for corporates, speculators and financial institutions alike.

3
Market Overview

3.1 GLOBAL MARKET

Simply defined, foreign exchange is the buying of one currency and the selling of another, always achieved in pairs. For example, the European euro against the American dollar (EUR/USD) or the dollar against the Japanese yen (USD/JPY). It is a global, over-the-counter market, which is unregulated and is in operation 24 hours a day, seven days a week. There are dealing centres in all the major capitals of the free world, from sunrise in Sydney, Tokyo and the rest of the Far East financial centres, through daytime trading activities in London and the European centres, across the Atlantic to New York and Chicago and on westwards to sunset in Los Angeles and Hawaii.

Individual buyers and sellers will generally deal verbally over the telephone, or act through brokers, or electronically. This means that rates change from dealer to dealer rather than being controlled by a central market. For example, investors do not call various dealers for the best price on a specific stock as the price is quoted on the stock exchange, but they do call different dealers to get the best exchange rate on a specific currency. They may also refer to various widely available bank/broker screens for indicative pricing (see Figure 3.1).

> The foreign exchange market has an average daily turnover of approximately $ 1.6 trillion and is the largest in the world.

3.2 NO PHYSICAL TRADING FLOOR

The market is decentralized with no physical trading floor. However, there are two exceptions to the lack of a physical marketplace. Firstly, foreign currency futures are traded on a few regulated markets, the better known of which are IMM in Chicago,

Quote Board 2 (filtered)			
▽ Symbol △	Bid	Ask	Description
AUD/CAD.fx	0.9284	0.9294	Aus Dollar/Canadian Dollar Spot
AUD/JPY.fx	97.15	97.20	Aus Dollar/Japanese Yen Spot
EUR/AUD.fx	1.6175	1.6185	Euro/Aus Dollar Spot
EUR/CHF.fx	1.5846	1.5850	Euro/Swiss Franc Spot
EUR/GBP.fx	0.7662	0.7665	Euro/GB Pound Spot
EUR/SGD.fx	2.1146	2.1166	Euro/Singapore Dollar Spot
EUR/USD.fx	1.5204	1.5207	Euro/US Dollar Spot
GBP/AUD.fx	2.1105	2.1120	GB Pound/Aus Dollar Spot
GBP/PLN.fx	4.5766	4.5966	GB Pound/Polish Zloty Spot
GBP/USD.fx	1.9839	1.9843	GB Pound/US Dollar Spot
USD/CAD.fx	0.9882	0.9887	US Dollar/Canadian Dollar Spot
USD/JPY.fx	103.40	103.43	US Dollar/Japanese Yen Spot
USD/ZAR.fx	7.7525	7.7775	US Dollar/SA Rand Spot

US Dollar/SA Rand Spot

Figure 3.1 This example of a broker screen shows 'live' market prices for major currencies against the dollar (e.g. dollar against Japanese yen (USD/JPY)) and cross-currencies (e.g. Australian dollar against the Canadian dollar (Aud/Cad). Reproduced by permission of GFT Global Markets. *Source:* GFT Global Markets

SIMEX in Singapore and LIFFE in London. Secondly, there are daily 'fixings' in some countries where major currency dealers meet to 'fix' the exchange rate of their local currency against currencies of their major trading partners, at a predetermined moment in the day. Immediately after the fixing, the rates continue to fluctuate and trade freely; for example, fixing the dollar against the Israeli shekel. However, fixings are occurring with less and less frequency and are simply becoming symbolic meetings.

Currency futures obligates its owner to purchase a specified asset at a specified exercise price on the contract maturity date

---

3.3 A 'PERFECT' MARKET

By dint of modern communications and information systems being dynamically available in all centres to all market participants, and the international applicability of the products traded, the foreign exchange market probably comes nearer than any of the global financial markets to being considered a 'perfect' market.

> **The foreign exchange market is a global network of buyers and sellers of currencies.**

The United Kingdom is, in effect, the geographic centre, with America a distant second and Japan in third place. Approximately 84 % of the world's foreign exchange business is executed in these three major dealing centres. Of course, there are also many smaller centres in different parts of the world – for example, Zurich, Frankfurt and Singapore. Perhaps the most important reason for London being in such a prominent position is its location among disparate time zones. During the day, at one time or another, London markets are in contact with European markets, several Asian and Middle East markets and major North American markets. Also, this leading position arises from the large volume of international business that is generated in London.

3.4   THE MAIN INSTRUMENTS

The main instruments for foreign exchange trading include both traditional products such as spot, forwards and swaps, and more exotic products such as currency options and currency swaps. The beauty of the foreign exchange market is its ability to accommodate new products – for instance, currency options come in all shapes and sizes, and can be tailor-made to serve any specific purpose.

The products used today are described as:

- **Spot** – A single outright transaction involving the exchange of two currencies at a rate agreed on the date of the contract for value or delivery (cash settlement) within two business days.
- **Forward** – A transaction involving the exchange of two currencies at a rate agreed on the date of the contract for value or delivery at some time in the future (more than two business days).
- **Swap** – A transaction which involves the actual exchange of two currencies (principle amount only) on a specific date, at a rate agreed at the time of conclusion of the contract (the short leg) and a reverse exchange of the same two currencies at a date further in the future, at a rate agreed at the time of the contract (the long leg).
- **Currency swap** – A contract that commits two counter parties to exchange streams of interest payments in different currencies for an agreed period of time, and to exchange principle amounts in different currencies at a pre-agreed exchange rate at maturity.

- **Currency option** – A contract, which gives the owner the right, but not the obligation, to buy or sell a currency with another currency at a specific rate during a specific period.
- **Foreign exchange futures** – This is a forward contract for standardized currency amounts and for standard value dates. Buyers and sellers of futures are required to post initial margin or security deposits for each contract and have to pay brokerage commissions.

3.5   THE DOLLAR'S ROLE

Approximately 86.3 %* of foreign exchange transactions have a dollar leg, amounting to over \$ 2.5 trillion per day. The dollar plays such a large role in the markets for the following reasons.

1. It is used as an investment currency throughout the world.
2. It is a reserve currency held by many central banks.
3. It is a transaction currency in many international commodity markets.
4. Monetary bodies use it as an intervention currency for operations in their own currencies.

3.6   WIDELY TRADED CURRENCY PAIRS

The most widely traded currency pairs are:

- the American dollar against the Japanese yen (USD/JPY);
- the European euro against the American dollar (EUR/USD);
- the British pound against the American dollar (GBP/USD); and
- the American dollar against the Swiss franc (USD/CHF).

Over the past few years, it should be noted that the currency composition of turnover has become more diversified with the share of the four largest currencies falling, although the US dollar/euro continues to be the most traded currency pair. The most notable increases in share were for the Australian and New Zealand dollars, which have attracted attention from investors as high-yielding currencies, and the Hong Kong dollar, which has benefited from being associated with the economic expansion of China. In addition, the share of emerging market currencies in total turnover has increased.

---

* *BIS Triennial Central Bank Survey of FX and Derivatives Market Activity in April 2007, published September and December 2007.*

Table 3.1 Global foreign exchange market turnover[1] (Daily averages in April, in billions of US dollars)

Instrument	1989	1995	2001	2004	2007
Spot transactions	317	494	387	621	1005
Outright forwards	27	97	131	208	362
Foreign exchange swaps	190	546	656	944	1714
Estimated gaps in reporting	56	53	26	107	129
Total 'traditional' turnover	**590**	**1190**	**1200**	**1880**	**3210**
Memorandum item: Turnover at April 2007 exchange rates[2]	570	1150	1420	1950	3210

[1] Adjusted for local and cross-border double-counting. Due to incomplete maturity breakdown, components do not always sum to totals.

[2] Non-US dollar legs of foreign currency transactions were converted into original currency amounts at average exchange rates for April of each survey year and then reconverted into US dollar amounts at average April 2007 exchange rates.

Source: BIS Triennial Central Bank Survey of FX and Derivatives Market Activity in April 2007, published September and December 2007.

Reproduced by permission of the Bank for International Settlement

In general, EUR/USD is by far the most traded currency pair and has captured approximately 27 %* of the global turnover. It is followed by USD/JPY with 13 % and GBP/USD with 12 % (see Tables 3.1 and 3.2). Of course, most national currencies are represented in the foreign exchange market, in one form or another. Most currencies operate under floating exchange rate mechanism against one another. The rates can rise or fall depending largely on economic, political and military situations in a given country.

3.7 CONCLUDING REMARKS

The foreign exchange market consists of a global network, where currencies are bought and sold 24 hours a day. What began as a way of facilitating trade across country borders has grown into one of the most liquid, hectic and volatile financial markets in the world – where the players have the potential to generate huge profits or losses.

Over the last few years, several important features of the evolution of the markets can be highlighted. Firstly, the average daily turnover has grown by an exceptional 71 % since April 2004, to approximately $ 3.2 trillion. Secondly, growth in turnover was broad-based across the foreign exchange instruments, with more than half of the

* *BIS Triennial Central Bank Survey of FX and Derivatives Market Activity in April 2007, published September and December 2007.*

Table 3.2 Reported foreign exchange turnover by currency pairs[1] (Daily averages in April, in billions of US dollars and percentages)

	2001		2004		2007	
Currency pair	Amount	% share	Amount	% share	Amount	% share
USD/EUR	354	30	501	28	840	27
USD/JPY	231	20	296	17	397	13
USD/GBP	125	11	245	14	361	12
USD/AUD	47	4	90	5	175	6
USD/CHF	57	5	78	4	143	5
USD/CAD	50	4	71	4	115	4
USD/Swedish krona[2]	–	–	–	–	56	2
USD/Oth	195	17	292	16	572	19
EUR/JPY	30	3	51	3	70	2
EUR/GBP	24	2	43	2	64	2
EUR/CHF	12	1	26	1	54	2
EUR/Oth	21	2	39	2	112	4
Other currency pairs	26	2	42	2	122	4
All currency pairs	**1173**	**100**	**1773**	**100**	**3081**	**100**

[1] Adjusted for local and cross-border double-counting.
[2] The US dollar/Swedish krona pair could not be separately identified before 2007 and is included in 'other'
Source: BIS Triennial Central Bank Survey of FX and Derivatives Market Activity in April 2007, published September and December 2007.
Reproduced by permission of the Bank for International Settlement

increase in turnover accounted for by the growth in foreign exchange swaps. One factor for this could be changes in hedging activity. In addition, growth in the turnover of outright forward contracts also picked up considerably. In contrast, turnover in the spot market was roughly unchanged from that in the previous three-year period. Thirdly, the composition of turnover by counterparty changed substantially. Transactions between reporting dealers and non-reporting financial institutions, such as hedge funds, mutual funds, pension funds and insurance companies, more than doubled between April 2004 and April 2007 and contributed more than half of the increase in aggregate turnover. Underlying factors included strong investor activity in an environment of trending exchange rates and low levels of financial market volatility, plus a shift among institutional investors with a longer-term investment horizon towards holding more internationally diversified portfolios and a marked increase in the levels of technical trading.

In addition, the currency composition of turnover has become more diversified over the past three years. The share of the four largest currencies fell, although the US dollar/euro continued to be the most traded currency pair. The most notable increases in share were for the Australian and New Zealand dollars, which have attracted attention from investors as high-yielding currencies, and the Hong Kong dollar, which has benefited from being associated with the economic expansion of China, with the share of emerging market currencies increasing.

Furthermore, the spread of electronic trading platforms has also contributed to turnover, in part because it has enabled large financial institutions to set-up algorithmic trading systems, and has additionally provided trading facilities to retail investors. The Bank for International Settlements survey found a significant increase in the participation by these investor groups, in particular by hedge funds in driving-up volumes, which was supported by substantial growth in the use of prime brokerage. The share of trade between reporting dealers and non-reporting financial institutions executed through electronic systems varies considerably across countries. For instance, it is estimated that electronic execution accounts for almost 60 % of turnover in Switzerland and around 50 % in Australia, Germany, Hong Kong and South Africa, while the median share is 32 %. Against this, the median share of electronic execution is 17 % for non-financial customers.

4
Major Participants

Participants in the foreign exchange market are many and varied and the individual involvement of each participant can vary dramatically. Surveys over recent years tend to indicate that participants can broadly be divided into three main groups: banks, brokers and clients. Commercial banks are by far the most active, while brokers act as intermediaries. Clients can be classed as anything from multinational corporations to individual investors to speculators. Who then are the active participants in this global market?

4.1 GOVERNMENTS

Governments sometimes have requirements for foreign currency. This may be for paying staff salaries and local bills of an embassy abroad, or for a foreign currency credit line, most often in dollars, to a third world national government for industrial or agricultural development. In its turn, the third world nation's government will periodically have to pay interest due on any foreign loans, with the capital sum eventually having to be repaid. It is more than likely that the Government would approach the market via its own central bank or a commercial bank.

Foreign exchange rates are of particular concern to governments because changes in foreign exchange rates affect the value of products and financial instruments. As a result, unexpected or large changes can affect the health of a nation's markets and financial systems. Exchange rate changes also impact a nation's international investment flow, as well as export and import prices. These factors, in turn, can influence inflation and economic growth.

For example, suppose the price of the Japanese yen moves from 120 yen per dollar to 110 yen per dollar over the course of a few weeks. In market jargon, the yen is 'strengthening', or becoming more expensive against the dollar. If the new exchange rate persists, it will lead to several related effects:

1. Japanese exports to America will become more expensive. Over time, this might cause export volumes to America to decline, which, in turn, might lead to job losses in Japan.
2. The higher American import prices might be an inflationary influence in America.
3. American exports to Japan will become less expensive, which might lead to an increase in American exports and a boost to American employment.

In addition, when governments get involved in the foreign exchange markets, they can either do so via their central banks or directly via market-making institutions. In general, governments will only get directly involved because of an economic need, for example establishing hedges on foreign funding, debt conversions or defense contracts.

4.2 BANKS

4.2.1 Central Banks

It goes without saying that the majority of developed market economies have a central bank whose role tends to be diverse and can differ from country to country and who are the traditional moderators of excess. Central banks are primarily the guardians of the national currencies and are usually responsible for setting monetary and exchange rate policy. Quite often, exchange rate policy is regarded as the outcome of monetary policy and the Bank of England, the European Central Bank, the Swiss National Bank, the Bank of Japan and, to a lesser extent, the Federal Reserve Bank will enter the market to correct what are felt to be unnecessarily large movements, often in conjunction with one another. By their actions, however, they can sometimes create the excesses they are specifically trying to prevent. In a practical sense, monitoring of the markets involves checking the prices dealt in the inter-bank market. However, sometimes, they even 'test' market prices by actually dealing in order to check the integrity of those quoted prices.

Central banks, whether they set foreign exchange policy on their own or follow orders of the finance minister, are the executing agency to implement that policy through a variety of tools, the most direct of which is buying or selling their currency. This intervention in the foreign exchange market will counter disorderly market conditions.

For example, two recent instances of intervention involved the sale of dollars for yen in June 1998 (Figure 4.1) and for euros in September 2000 (Figure 4.2).

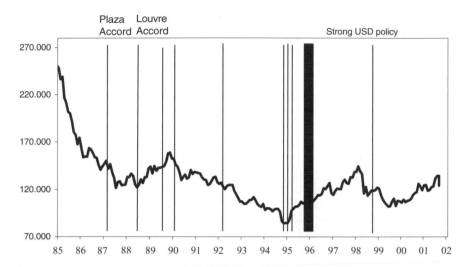

Figure 4.1 G7 Intervention: US dollars for Japanese Yen (1998). Reproduced by permission of Standard & Poor's. *Source:* MMS

Intervention, in general, does not shift the balance of supply and demand immediately. Instead, intervention affects the present and future behaviour of investors. In this regard, intervention is used as a device to signal a desired exchange rate movement.

The second group of banks can best be described as aggressive managers of their reserves. Some of the Middle Eastern and Far Eastern central banks fall into

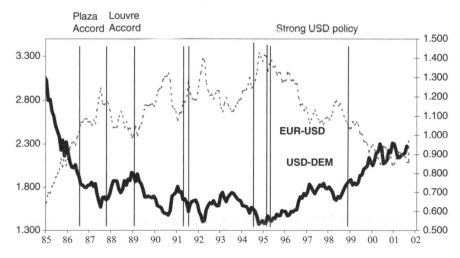

Figure 4.2 G7 Intervention: US dollars for European euros (2000). Reproduced by permission of Standard & Poor's. *Source:* MMS

this category. They are major speculative risk takers and their activities often disturb market equilibrium. Alongside this activity, the central banks have clients in their own right and they will have commercial transactions to undertake. In certain countries, central banks are involved in local fixing sessions between commercial banks, often acting as an adjudicator to the correct fixing of the daily rates, or to ensure that the supply and demand for foreign currency is balanced at a rate that is in line with its current monetary policy.

4.2.2   Trading Banks

Banks (trading banks), whether large or small, deal with each other in the 'interbank market', where they are obliged to make a 'two-way price', i.e. to quote a bid and an offer (a buy and a sell price). This category is perhaps the largest and includes international, commercial and trade banks. The bulk of today's trading activity is concentrated between 100 and 200 banks world wide, out of a possible 2000 dealer participants. These banks also deal with their clients, some of the more important of which also qualify for two-way prices. In the vast majority of cases, however, most corporations will only be quoted according to their particular requirement. These banks rely on the knowledge of the market and their expertise in assessing trends in order to take advantage of them for speculative gain.

4.2.3   Commercial Banks

Commercial banks (clearing banks in the UK) operate as international banks in the foreign exchange market, as do many retail banks in other major dealing centres. Many banks in the UK have specialized regional branches to cater for all their clients' foreign business, including foreign exchange. All this retail business will eventually be channelled through to the bank's City of London foreign exchange dealing room for consolidation with other foreign currency positions either for market cover or continued monitoring by the specialist dealing-room personnel.

The situation in America is slightly different, where legislation prohibits banks in certain states from maintaining branch networks, but all banks have their affiliates or preferred agents in the main dealing centres of New York, Chicago and Los Angles.

Other commercial banks have large amounts of foreign exchange business to transact on behalf of their clients, and although they will have their own dealing rooms, for one reason or another they have not developed their operations to become involved in the interbank foreign exchange markets.

4.2.4   Regional or Correspondent Banks

Regional or correspondent banks do not make a market or carry positions and, in fact, turn to the larger money centre banks to offset their risk. Such relationships have been built up over many years of reciprocal service, and in many instances are mutual, whereby the correspondent bank abroad acts as the clearing agent in its own currency for the other bank involved.

4.2.5 Investment and Merchant Banks

The strength of investment and merchant banks lies in their corporate finance and capital markets activities, which have been developed over many years' servicing the financial needs of large corporations, rather than retail clients. With the multi-currency sophistication of the capital markets and the wide international spread of corporations and other market participants, they are frequently required to transact foreign exchange business, which they effect either by dealing direct or through the brokers' market.

It is important to note that today, the delineation between commercial and investment banks has blurred, and, hence the market activities of the two types of institutions are no longer clearly characterized.

4.3 BROKERING HOUSES

Brokering houses exist primarily to bring buyer and seller together at a mutually agreed price, acting as an agent in the same way that a stockbroker acts in the equities market, except that their activities are confined to acting between interbank market participants and they do not accept orders from corporate clients. The broker is not allowed to take a position in a currency and must act purely as a liaison. For this service, they receive a commission from both sides of the transaction, which will vary according to currency handled and from centre to centre.

The value to the banks of this service is that it is usually done quickly and it allows the bank to avoid having to deal on a competitor's price and paying the spread on the transaction. However, the use of live brokers has decreased in recent years, due mostly to the rise of the various interbank electronic brokerage systems, cutting out the need for human handling of the orders.

4.4 INTERNATIONAL MONETARY MARKET

The International Monetary Market (IMM) in Chicago trades currencies for contract amounts, which are relatively small in size and for only four specific maturities a year. Originally designed for the small investor, the IMM has grown apace since the early 1970s, and the major banks, whose original attitude was somewhat jaundiced, now find that it pays to keep in touch with developments on the IMM, which is often a market leader (Figures 4.3 and 4.4).

IMM Commitment of Traders - 'speculative positions'

w/e 19 Feb 2008

☐ The latest release of the IMM data covering speculative (non-commercial) futures market positioning on Feb 19 shows a very similar picture to last week's, i.e. a slight increase in implied USD shorts mainly due another rise in MXN longs which now look very overextended and further improvement in AUD bullish sentiment.

☐ There was a modest increase in EUR net longs as some of the immediate ECB easing fears eased while USD sentiment began to wane again. Hawkish BoE talk helped temper some of the pessimism on GBP although the speculators are still net short. Appetite for JPY remained strong despite a lot of interest in the high yielders, suggesting that while 'carry trade' may be back, it certainly looks different on the funding side. CHF lacked interest either way.

☐ The RBA tide has been lifting all the commodity currency boats for several weeks, but this time yet another rise in net AUD longs contrasted with small declines in NZD and CAD net longs. This suggests that while the overall risk appetite has probably increased, speculators are still keeping a fair amount of capital on the sidelines. VS

Figure 4.3   IMM commitment of traders (USD/CAD). Reproduced by permission of 4CAST Limited. *Source:* 4castweb.com

4.5   MONEY MANAGERS

Money managers tend to be large New York commission houses and are frequently very aggressive players in the foreign exchange market. They act on behalf of their clients, but often deal on their own account. They are not limited to one time zone, but deal around the world through their agents as each centre becomes operational.

4.6   CORPORATIONS

Corporations are, in the final analysis, the real end users of the foreign exchange market. With the exception only of the central banks that alter liquidity by means of their intervention, it is the corporate players by and large who affect supply and demand. When the other major players enter the market to buy and sell currencies, they do so not because they have a need, but in the hope of a quick and profitable return. The corporates, however, by coming to the market to offset currency exposure, permanently change the liquidity of the currencies being dealt with.

4.7   FUND MANAGERS

These participants in the foreign exchange market are in the simplest form international and domestic money managers. They tend to deal in very large quantities as

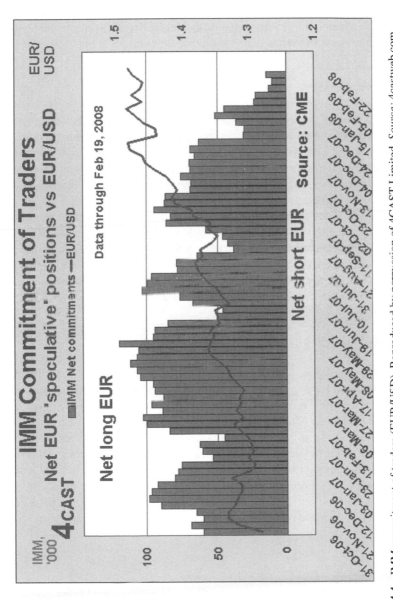

Figure 4.4 IMM commitment of traders (EUR/USD). Reproduced by permission of 4CAST Limited. *Source:* 4castweb.com

their pools of investment funds tend to be very large. Briefly, fund managers invest money across a range of countries and class of investments, depending on their investment charters and obligations to their investors, seeking the best investment opportunities for their funds. Investors range across the whole spectrum from pension funds to individual investors to governments. As has been shown in recent surveys, fund managers have come to exert a greater influence on currency trends and movements.

4.8   HEDGE FUNDS

Hedge funds can be described as a special class of fund manager and have come to be referred to by their more appropriate name of 'absolute return funds'. They are generally more concerned with managing the total risk of a pooled investment, than just relative performance. Hedge funds tend to be far more aggressive in their investment approaches and are more likely to be found borrowing to realize leverage potential with the added impulse of exploiting the use of derivatives.

Today, hedge funds lead the volumes in algorithmic foreign exchange and now account for the highest buy-side volume and strongest rate of growth. They place huge directional bets on currencies and their activities can be reflected in the overall rise and fall of foreign exchange trading volumes. For example, in early 2006 a lack of trends and an inability to read market price movements had a negative impact on hedge fund performance, slowing the pace of rising volumes.

4.9   RETAIL CLIENTS

Alongside these corporates, there is a none-too-significant volume from retail clients. This category includes many smaller companies, hedge funds, companies specializing in investment services linked to foreign currency funds or equities, fixed income brokers, the financing of aid programmes by registered worldwide charities and private individuals. With the rise in popularity of online equity investing, and a corresponding rise in online fixed income investing, it was only a matter of time before the average retail investor began to see opportunities in the foreign exchange market. Retail investors have been able to trade foreign exchange using highly leveraged margin accounts. The amount of trading, both in total volume and in individual trade amounts, remains low and is certainly dwarfed by the corporate and interbank markets.

4.10   OTHERS

Other financial institutions involved in the foreign exchange market include:

* stockbrokers;
* commodity firms;

- insurance companies;
- charities and private institutions;
- private individuals.

4.11   SPECULATORS

All the above tend to have some sort of underlying exposure that has to be covered. Speculators, however, have no underlying exposure to hedge, rather they attempt to fulfil the adage 'buy low, sell high' by trading for trading profit alone. Foreign exchange is an ideal speculative tool, offering volatility, liquidity and easy margin or leverage. This activity is vital to the stability of the markets. Without speculation, hedgers would find the market too illiquid to accommodate their needs (Figure 4.5).

While speculators seek excess profits as a reward for their activities, the process of speculating itself drives the markets towards lower volatility and price stability. No modern commodity, equity or debt market could operate without the speculators. It is estimated that up to 90 % of the daily volume of trading activity in the foreign exchange markets is a result of speculator activity, with the balance primarily made up of commercial hedging transactions.

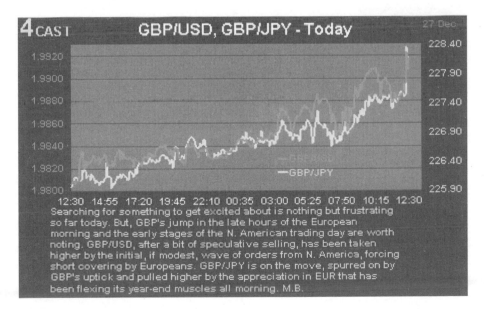

Figure 4.5 Daily forecast of USD/CAD, EUR/USD flows: speculators are caught by low liquidity and real money buyer. Reproduced by permission of 4CAST Limited. *Source:* 4castweb.com

4.12   TRADE AND FINANCIAL FLOWS

The foreign exchange market provides the liquidity for all these market participants to convert their trade and financial flows from the currency of one money centre to the currency of another. These participants buy and sell foreign exchange directly or indirectly from the interbank market, which comprises professional foreign exchange traders who operate in every financial centre of the world.

These flows and the products available to facilitate these conversions are shown in Figure 4.6. The products – the majority of which have been developed for the clients of the foreign exchange market rather than for professional traders – are also used to hedge or protect the values of cash flows, as these can be affected by the potential changes in the relationships of the currencies involved. The funds borrowed or invested in the money markets may also need to be hedged for the same reasons.

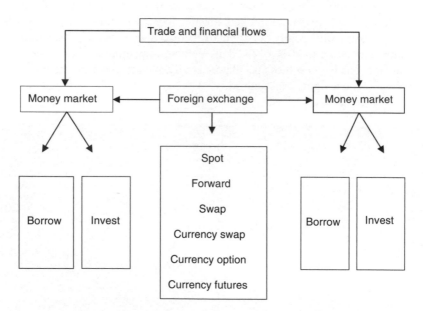

Figure 4.6   Financial flows and available products

5
Roles Played

To make a market means to be willing and ready to buy and sell currencies.

5.1 MARKET MAKERS

Market makers are those market participants that buy *and* sell currencies. As market makers, dealers (or traders) generally, according to market practice, quote a two-way price to another market maker, but not to most corporations.

> **The terms 'dealer' and 'trader' are used interchangeably when referring to market makers.**

For market makers, reciprocity is standard practice. They constantly make prices to one another. Market makers are primarily major banks, for example, Barclays, HSBC, J.P. Morgan Chase, Morgan Stanley, Deutsche Bank, Union Bank of Switzerland and Citibank.

5.2 PRICE TAKERS

Price takers are those market participants who seek to either buy or sell currencies. They are usually corporations and fund managers (investors). For price takers, there is no reciprocity inasmuch as they won't quote prices back to the other market participants.

5.3   A NUMBER OF ROLES

The major participants in the market play a number of roles depending on their need for foreign exchange and the purpose of their activities:

- International money centre banks are market makers and deal with other market participants.
- Regional banks deal with market makers to meet their own foreign exchange needs and those of their clients.
- Central banks are in the market to handle foreign exchange transactions for their governments, for certain state-owned entities and for other central banks. They also pay or receive currencies not usually held in reserves and stabilize markets through intervention.
- Investment banks, like money centre banks, can be market makers and deal with other market participants.
- Corporations are generally price takers and usually enter into a foreign exchange transaction for a specific purpose, such as to convert trade or capital flows or to hedge a currency position.
- Brokers are the intermediaries or middlemen in the market, and as such do not take positions on their own behalf. They act as a mechanism for matching deals between market makers. Brokers provide market makers with a bid and/or offer quote that has been left with them by other market makers. Brokers are bound by confidentiality not to reveal the name of one client to another until after a deal has been completed.
- Investors are usually managers of large investment funds and are a major force in moving exchange rates. They may engage in the market for hedging, investment and/or speculation.
- Regulatory authorities, while not actually participants in the market, impact the market from time to time. Regulatory authorities include government and international bodies. Most of the market is self-regulated, with guidelines of conduct being established by groups such as the Bank for International Settlements (the BIS) and the International Monetary Fund (IMF). National governments can and do impose controls on foreign exchange by legislation or market intervention through the central banks.
- Speculators seek excess profits as a reward for their activities.

CONCLUDING REMARKS

All of the above activities can be undertaken by a variety of market participants. For example, banks may be market makers most of the time, but for some of the time they can also be hedgers or speculators.

6
Purposes

The participants in the foreign exchange markets effect transactions for various purposes, principally arising from the need to cover or hedge other financial or commercial operations, although in practice it is sometimes difficult to draw a clear line between these categories. For example, covering and hedging operations may well contain elements of speculation. Whatever the nature of the transaction, they are initiated by the banks' clients or by banks themselves for their own account.

6.1 TRANSACTIONS

The following are examples of those types of transaction, undertaken by all categories of market participants, which are commonplace in the foreign exchange market today.

6.1.1 Commercial Transactions

For commercial transactions, manufacturing companies who buy in raw materials from abroad and export finished products undertake both purchases and sales of foreign exchange, always dependent upon the companies' domicile and the currency used for invoicing.

Importers of goods, whether acting as principals or intermediaries, will undertake purchases of foreign currency. Contractors involved in overseas projects will be market participants as both buyers and sellers of foreign currency. Also, international insurance, shipping, air transport and travel companies have need of frequent involvement in the market, as do any other individuals or companies offering services overseas.

6.1.2   Funding

Banks and multinational corporations require specific wholesale funding for their commercial loan or other foreign investment portfolios, alongside day-to-day funding requirements of their net currency cash flows.

6.1.3   Hedging

The hedging of any open currency exposure is frequently better handled through off-balance sheet products, such as currency options, which ultimately will have an effect on the foreign exchange market. Also, companies involved in direct commercial investment overseas, the purchase and maintenance of plant and materials, or those financing operations of foreign based subsidiaries, will be frequent participants in the market, as will property companies or individuals involved in the purchase and sale of property overseas. They may seek foreign currency financing or may convert local currency funding via the foreign exchange market.

6.1.4   Portfolio Investment

Added to this group are banks and other entities involved in portfolio investment overseas, or dealing in foreign securities, who will, for position establishment and profit realization purposes, be both buyers and sellers of foreign currencies.

6.1.5   Personal

On the personal transaction front, tourists, immigrants and emigrants making outward and inward remittances in foreign currency make up the bulk of the volume, if not the value, of retail foreign exchange business transacted in the market. Royalties, commissions, patents and copyrights from abroad will also be transacted in the market.

6.2   MARKET MAKING

Market-making transactions by international banks is also the reason for being involved in the foreign exchange market, and taking this role a stage further, the trading banks will seek to position themselves against anticipated currency movements. Positions can be set up defensively in the light of the banks' known immediate (or future) requirements, or opportunistically, with dealers looking for a short-term gain. Today, there are many intra-day traders who will close all long- and short-cash positions at the end of the trading day.

6.3 FOREIGN EXCHANGE EXPOSURE

As mentioned previously, many organizations are at risk to the financial impact of the market due to changes in foreign exchange rates. In particular, there are three types of foreign exchange exposure:

> **Foreign exchange exposure is the risk of financial impact due to changes in foreign exchange rates.**

6.3.1 Transaction Exposure

Transaction exposure principally impacts a company's profit and loss and cash flow. It results from transacting business in a currency that is different from the currency of the company's home base. Companies face transaction exposure when they import or export goods and services denominated in foreign currencies, or when they borrow or invest in foreign currencies.

For example, when a small Irish vitamin company, a subsidiary of a large Dublin-based food conglomerate, imports cod liver oil from Sweden, it is invoiced in Swedish krona. Payment is due on delivery of the oil in three months, but in the next two weeks the food manufacturer has to fix the pricing levels and send a profit and loss forecast for the next six months to the treasurer of the parent company. The company has a transaction exposure because they have a risk that the Swedish krona will strengthen against the euro by the time the payment is due, making the cost of goods in euros greater than the company anticipated and possibly eroding their profit margins.

Of course, this exposure could be eliminated or mitigated through the use of foreign exchange products, such as a forward contract, which could lock in a specific exchange rate for settlement at the time the payment is due.

6.3.2 Translation Exposure

Translation exposure principally impacts a company's balance sheet and results from the translation of foreign assets and liabilities into the company's home currency for accounting purposes. This occurs when the financial statements of a company's foreign subsidiaries are consolidated into the parent's statements and translated into the parent's reporting base currency. (Transaction and translation exposure occasionally overlap).

For example, a Swiss food company has an American subsidiary in the sweet business. The subsidiary company had an asset value of 52.5 million Swiss francs (or $ 35 million) at the beginning of the year, when the exchange rate was Sfr 1.50 per $ 1. There was no change in the asset value of the subsidiary during the year due to operational reasons. In that time, however, the Swiss franc strengthened to Sfr 1.43

per $1. The asset value of the sweet company on the Swiss company's balance sheet has dropped to Sfr 50 050 000 ($35 million at 1.43) a loss of Sfr 2 450 000 (52 500 000 minus 50 050 000), simply from the translation of the Swiss company's long-term investment in the American sweet company from dollars to Swiss francs.

Again, this exposure can be eliminated or mitigated through the use of foreign exchange products such as a forward contract or a currency option.

6.3.3 Economic Exposure

Economic exposure relates to a company's exposure to foreign markets and suppliers. It can also be referred to as competitive, strategic or operational exposure and is more difficult to identify. In fact, identification of economic exposure involves in-depth forecasting to determine how sensitive the company's business is to changes in exchange rates. It recognizes that the value of a company is impacted by changes in the exchange rate on both its current and future products and markets. For instance, a company has foreign exchange exposure arising from payables and receivables that are not yet booked but will most probably occur. As these exposures cannot receive hedge accounting treatment, they are a problem for companies.

An example often cited in discussing economic exposure is that of a major American film manufacturer whose main competitor in most of its markets is a large Japanese Company. The American company has an active exchange rate risk – management programme, which recognizes that when the value of the yen rises against the dollar – say, from an exchange rate of 150 to 140 – the American film becomes more competitive with the Japanese film in Japanese markets, and the Japanese film becomes less competitive with the American film in American markets. When the yen weakens against the dollar – say, from an exchange rate of 140 to 150 – it has the opposite competitive impact.

Again, however, available products in the foreign exchange market can address any problems with economic exposure.

CONCLUDING REMARKS

Today, there are products available in the foreign exchange market that can address all types of foreign exchange exposures and purposes. As mentioned in an earlier chapter, there are six basic foreign exchange products:

- spot transactions;
- forward contracts;
- foreign exchange swaps;
- currency swaps;
- currency options; and
- foreign exchange futures contracts.

Part II
Foreign Exchange Products

7
Spot Foreign Exchange

Foreign exchange rates are a means of expressing the value and worth of an economy by its currency *vis-à-vis* that of another. Normal market usage is to quote the exchange rate for **spot value**, i.e. for *delivery two business days from the trade date* (except Canadian transactions against the dollar, when the spot date is only one day). The two business days are normally required in order to enable the trade information between the counterparties involved to be agreed and to process the funds through the local clearing systems. The two payments are made on the same date, regardless of the time zone difference (see Figure 7.1).

7.1 SPOT AND RECIPROCAL RATES

The rate used in a spot deal is the **spot rate** and is the price at which one currency can be bought or sold, expressed in terms of the other currency, for delivery on the spot value date.

> **The ratio at which one currency is exchanged for another for settlement in two business days (value date) is called the spot exchange rate.**

The spot exchange rate can be expressed in either currency, thus this price has two parts, the base currency and the equivalent number of units of the other currency. For example, a rate for the US dollar against the Swiss franc would be quoted as 1.6703. This means there are 1.6703 Swiss francs to 1 dollar. When one rate is known, the spot exchange rate expressed in the other currency (the **reciprocal**) is easily calculated. The price of 1 dollar, expressed in Swiss francs, is 1/$ 0.5986 or Sfr 1.6703. Although some newspapers calculate and publish both exchange rates, it has become a standard market practice among traders to quote the foreign exchange for most currencies as

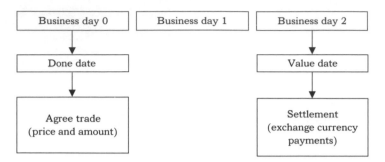

Figure 7.1   Example of a foreign exchange transaction

the amount of foreign currency that will be exchanged for 1 dollar. For example, if a bank trader was asked to quote a rate for Swiss francs against the dollar, the response would most probably be sfr 1.6703 rather than $0.5986. In this case, 1 dollar is the traded commodity and the trader is quoting the price in Swiss francs. This type of quotation is known as 'European terms'.

7.2   EUROPEAN AND AMERICAN TERMS

Normally, the accepted practice is to quote in **indirect** or **European terms**. The price in dollar terms signifies how many dollars a single unit of the foreign currency is worth. In this case, the foreign currency is the **fixed currency** and the dollar is the **variable currency**. However, there are exceptions to this rule. In contrast, the European euro, the British pound, the Australian and New Zealand dollar, and some other old British area currencies, such as the Maltese pound, are quoted as the number of American dollars to the currency. This is an overhang from the days when these currencies were primarily quoted against sterling and therefore adopted the same quoting convention as sterling against the dollar. In this case, the currencies are always expressed in **American** or **direct terms**. For example, if a Swiss franc against the dollar price is expressed, it would read SFR 1.67/$1 or $1 equals SFR 1.67. This means that it costs SFR 1.67 to buy $1. The American dollar is the fixed currency and the Swiss franc is the variable currency. Alternatively, if a dollar against sterling price is expressed, it would read $1.43/£1 or £1 equals $1.43. This means that it costs $1.43 to buy £1. The pound is the fixed currency and the dollar is the variable currency.

> An American term is merely the reciprocal of the rate derived using European terms.

Thus, the usage of either European terms or American terms is based on market practices. A market trader would quote pounds sterling as $ 1.5310 per pound and euros as $ 0.9940 per euro. This distinction is critical to understanding foreign exchange quotes and dealing screens. For example, when a corporate treasurer telephones a bank asking for foreign exchange quotes, the trader will assume that the treasurer understands market conventions and will quickly rattle off prices for different currencies in the customary European or American terms.

7.3 SPOT TRANSACTIONS

7.3.1 Bid–Offer Spreads

Foreign currency traders are considered to be dealers when they make a two-way market price, i.e. not just quoting one rate but two.

> **A bid is a price at which a trader is willing to buy a currency and an offer is a price at which a trader is willing to sell a currency.**

A sample of two-way quotes is:.

EUR/USD	0.9945–0.9948
USD/JPY	118.53–118.56
USD/CHF	1.6703–1.6708

Like other financial markets, the spread favours the dealer who buys currency at one price and sells it at a slightly higher price. To determine whether a trade will take place at the dealer's bid or offer rate, a corporate treasurer must first know the currency in which the dealer is bidding or offering. That is, whether the transaction is quoted in European terms such that the traded commodity is 1 dollar, or in American terms, such that the traded commodity in 1 unit of foreign currency.

7.3.2 Reading Foreign Exchange Rates

For example, the dollar against the Swiss franc could be quoted as 1.6703/08. But what does this quote actually indicate? As has been mentioned, a market maker will normally quote a two-way price – in other words, it is obliged to make a bid and an offer for dollars against, in this case, the Swiss franc. Market makers will always quote to their advantage and to the other person's disadvantage. The left-hand side of the quote (1.6703) is the quoting person's bid for dollars, obviously surrendering as few Swiss francs as possible. Conversely, the right-hand side of the quote (1.6708) is the market maker's offer for dollars, at which they will ask for as many Swiss francs as possible. The difference between the rate at which someone will buy a currency and the rate at which that person will sell is called the **profit** (spread).

For example, when a market maker quotes spot Swiss franc (against the dollar), the trader will say:

'dollar/Swiss franc is 1.6703–1.6708'

where their bid is at Sfr 1.6703/$ 1 and their offer is at Sfr 1.6708/$ 1. That is, the market maker will buy $ 1 for Sfr 1.6703, which means the client will sell $ 1 for Sfr 1.6703 – the client sells at the market maker's bid. Conversely, the market maker will sell $ 1 for Sfr 1.6708, which means the client will buy $ 1 for Sfr 1.6708 – the client buys at the market maker's offer (see Figure 7.2).

It is important to remember that in any foreign exchange transaction, each party is both buying and selling, since it is buying one currency while selling another. One way of determining which is the buying rate and which is the selling rate, is to remember that a market maker will buy dollars for another currency at a low rate (its bid rate) and sell dollars for another currency at a high rate (its offered rate). For currencies like sterling and euro, the market maker will buy sterling for dollars at the bid rate and sell sterling for dollars at the offered rate.

7.3.3   Big Figures

Usually, market makers will quote only the last two numbers in the prices, for example 03/08, thus assuming the other party knows the rest of the price, which is known as

Market maker		Market maker	
Sell francs	Buy francs	Sell dollars	Buy dollars
Buy dollars	Sell dollars	Buy sterling	Sell sterling
1.6703	1.6708	1.4395	1.4400
Buy francs	Sell francs	Buy dollars	Sell dollars
Sell dollars	Buy dollars	Sell sterling	Sell sterling
Market user		Market user	

Figure 7.2   Example of a currency transaction

the big figure, in this case 1.67. In an example of, say sterling/dollar being quoted 1.4397–1.4402, the big figure is both 1.43 and 1.44. However, in this case, the trader would say:

'97–02, around 1.44'

7.3.4   Spread

As mentioned above, by quoting a higher offer than bid, the market maker ensures that if both sides of the quote are dealt on simultaneously, the market maker will profit from the difference between the bid and offer. This difference is the **spread** and the size of the spread is affected by various factors. The main factors are the assessment of risk, the volatility of the market, the liquidity of the currency, and the time of the day in each time zone.

7.4   DIRECT VERSUS BROKERED DEALING

When a dealer calls another dealer for a price, it is called **direct dealing**. When a dealer puts a bid or offer in at a foreign exchange broker or via some Internet trading platforms, it is called **brokered dealing**. Brokered dealing is somewhat like a silent auction as the buyers and sellers are unaware of each other's identity until the deal is done, and the bid and offer process may not be accepted.

7.5   CROSS RATES

> A cross-rate is the rate of exchange between two currencies that do not involve the domestic currency. In the international market, cross rates have come to mean rates that do not involve the American dollar.

Most transactions are dealt in American terms. However, currencies are also dealt against each other; for example, the Swiss franc against the Japanese yen (SFR/JPY). In these instances, it is necessary to calculate the **cross rate**.

In order to calculate this cross rate, start with the two rates against the dollar. The objective is to obtain the number of Japanese yen per Swiss franc. Consider:

One dollar = francs 1.6703/08
One dollar = yen 121.70/75

Each quotation represents a bid and an offer for the currency against the dollar. The cross rate is achieved by taking opposite sides of the two prices. The rate for selling yen and buying francs is achieved by using the left-hand side of the dollar/yen (bid) rate and the right-hand side of the dollar/franc (offer) rate. The same logic is applied for buying yen and selling francs. Thus, the above quotations can be broken down as follows:

$$121.70 \text{ divided by } 1.6708 = 72.84$$
$$121.75 \text{ divided by } 1.6703 = 72.89$$

Hence, the spot cross rate for Swiss francs against the Japanese yen is 72.84/89. The number of places after the decimal point is determined by the convention of the quoted currency (the variable currency). In the above example, this is the yen, since we are looking for the number of yen per franc. It is usual to quote cross-currency exchange rates using the 'heavier' currency as the base, for example the number of yen per franc.

There is, of course, a variation to the rule. For currencies like the euro and sterling, it is market practice to multiply the respective currencies against each other. For example, consider the following;

$$\text{One dollar} = \text{yen } 121.70/75$$
$$\text{One pound} = \text{dollar } 1.4330/35$$

Then the sterling against yen spot cross rate calculation will be:

$$121.70 \times 1.4330 \text{ and } 121.75 \times 1.4335 = 174.38/53$$

Thus it follows, that 1 pound is equal to 174.38 or 174.53 yen. This is the only way it is expressed.

7.6   PRICE DETERMINANTS

Exchange rates (or prices) in the foreign exchange market are driven by the laws of supply and demand. The supply and demand for specific currencies change, given the amount of trade and investment being done in that currency. If there is a high demand for a currency, its value increases. If there is a low demand then its value decreases.

However, exchange rates are not only affected by supply and demand. The exchange rate will also be influenced by the economic, political, monetary and social factors of the country involved and also by outside developments. Exchange rates can change quickly and significantly, reflecting the volatility in the market; and rates can also be moved by rumours and anticipated factors. Typically, currency rates can fluctuate from day-to-day due to small imbalances in supply and demand, and to economic and political factors that affect the sentiment of market makers and investors.

7.7 USES FOR SPOT TRANSACTIONS

Client groups, such as corporations, investors, funds and institutions, will use spot transactions as part of their foreign exchange management programmes. Speculators will also, use this market because it is extremely active and liquid with roughly two-thirds of all foreign exchange activity being traded. There can be plenty of movement (volatility) in any one day, which will enable a speculator to possibly benefit from such gyrations.

7.7.1 Risk consideration

It must be remembered that there are risks with spot transactions. Firstly, there is a **credit risk**. Like the risk a bank incurs when making a loan, a foreign exchange contract poses the risk that the client will not perform according to the terms of the contract (i.e. will not deliver the appropriate currency on time). In a foreign exchange

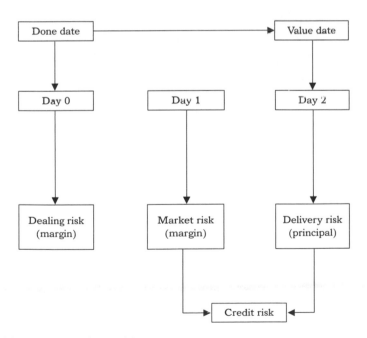

Figure 7.3 The spot exchange risk

transaction, the market maker and the client agree that each will deliver to the other a specified amount of a currency on a specific date, at an agreed rate. Trading the currencies of countries that are in different time zones compounds the risk.

Secondly, there is a **market/price risk**. Trading in any currency has a degree of risk. Exchange rate risk is inevitable because currency values rise and fall constantly in response to market pressures. When engaging in a foreign exchange trade, the client's position is open until it is closed or covered. While that position is open, the client is exposed to the risk of changes in exchange rates. A few moments can transform a potentially profitable transaction into a loss.

Thirdly, there is a **country risk**. Some countries (and their currencies) are more risky than others. Country risk may be due to anything from governmental regulations and restrictions to political situations, or the amount of foreign currency reserves the country holds. However, this risk is usually of less significance.

The spot exchange risk is shown graphically in Figure 7.3.

8
Forward Contracts

8.1 INTEREST RATE DIFFERENTIALS

Forwards work much like spots, but the value date is different from the spot date and usually extends further into the future, for example, six months from the commencement date. At first sight there would seem to be no reason why the spot and the forward rate should not be the same. However, one of the factors influencing a currency's forward exchange rate is the level of interest rates for that currency relative to interest rates in the other currency. There are many theories on how a forward exchange rate can be calculated, but market participants adopt the interest rate differential between two currencies and the current market spot rate as the basis of their calculations. The forward price is often referred to as **forward points, forward pips** or **swap points** (pips).

> **A forward contract (or forward outright) is a transaction executed today in which one currency is bought or sold against another for delivery on a specified date that is not the spot date, for example three months from the commencement date.**
>
> **Forward points are relative interest rate differentials expressed as units of currency, or fractions of the spot value of that currency.**

For example, assume that the spot and forward rates between dollars and sterling are the same, but the interest rates in sterling are 4 % per annum for a 3-month deposit, while in dollars they are 2 %. Investors would sell their dollars and buy sterling spot for the higher yield. They would simultaneously sell sterling and buy dollars forward for delivery at the end of the investment period. In this way, the investor would end up with more dollars than if the investment had been kept in dollars.

8.2   PERIODS

Market makers regularly trade forward contracts for periods of one, two, three, six and twelve months from the spot value date. A **broken date** or **odd date** forward deal is a contract with maturity other than a normal market quote of complete months. An example would be to ask for the forward pips for 24 days.

8.3   PREMIUM OR DISCOUNT

Forward contract prices are determined by two main factors: the current spot price between the two currencies and the interest rate prevailing in each of the two currencies. The forward price is calculated as the spot rate plus or minus the forward pips. To decide whether to add or subtract the forward pips, firstly determine whether the currency to be bought or sold is trading at a premium or is trading at a discount. As all exchange rates have a fixed and a variable component, if the interest rates in the variable currency are greater than those of the fixed currency, the variable currency is trading at a **discount** relative to the fixed currency and forward pips are added to the spot rate to obtain the forward rate. If the interest rates in the variable currency are less than those of the fixed currency, the variable currency is trading at a **premium** and forward pips are subtracted from the spot rate to obtain the forward rate.

There are two simple rules of thumb to decide if a currency is at a premium or a discount, and what to do with the forward points. Remember, exchange rates are quoted as units of that currency, which equal 1 dollar (except for sterling, euro and a few other currencies, such as the Australian and New Zealand dollars).

If the forward points are *ascending*, i.e. the offer is numerically higher than the bid (20/25), that is, if the forward points rise from left to right, the currency is at a discount to the dollar and, hence, the forward points are **added** to the spot rate. (The major exception is sterling and the euro, where they are at a premium to the dollar.) If the bid is numerically higher than the offer, i.e. the points are *descending* (25/20), i.e. the forward points decline from left to right, the currency is at a premium to the dollar and the forward points are **deducted** from the spot rate. (The major exception is the quotation for the euro and sterling against the dollar, where if the forward points decline from left to right, the points are *deducted*, but the dollar is at a premium to the euro and sterling.)

An example of how forward rates for the euro and Swiss franc might appear on an information screen or brokers screen is shown in Table 8.1. Note how the forward points decline from left to right and hence the forward points are deducted from the spot. It is common for the interest rates to be shown for the currency as well.

8.4   CALCULATIONS

Forward rates are not determined by where the market expects the currency to be in the future, but rather by the interest rate differential. Also, the forward exchange rate

Table 8.1 Example of deposit and forward points for the euro

09.09	EUR deposits		EUR forwards
06.41	3.25/3.4	o/n	−0.430/−0.405
08.04	3.26/3.41	t/n	−0.45/−0.41
08.06	3.28/3.34	s/n	−3.02/−2.97
08.56	3.31/3.37	1 month	−13.95/−13.80
08.56	3.34/3.39	2 months	−27.10/−26.90
09.00	3.36/3.42	3 months	−40.60/−40.30
09.00	3.39/3.45	6 months	−82.50/−81.50
09.00	3.45/3.51	9 months	−120.05/−118.05
09.00	3.56/3.62	12 months	−150.99/−147.99

Note: For explanation of o/n, t/n and s/n see Chapter 9.

is fixed at the time of the transaction, but no accounts are credited or debited until the maturity date.

The forward pips are calculated in the following way. If we assume that the spot and forward rates between dollars and sterling are the same, say 1.4400/10, but the interest rates in sterling are 4 % per annum for a 3-month deposit, while in dollars they are 2 % per annum for the same deposit, investors would sell their dollars and buy sterling spot for the higher yield. They would simultaneously sell sterling and buy dollars forward for delivery at the end of the investment period. In this way, the investors would end up with more dollars than if the money had been kept in dollars. For example, if Mr Jones has $ 5 million to invest for three months, at 2 %, the interest earned at the end of the period will be:

$$\frac{5\,000\,000 \times 92 \times 2}{360 \times 100} = \$25\,555.56$$

Thus, the total principle and interest earned at the end of the period will be $ 5 025 555.56 ($ 5 000 000 + $ 25 555.56).

However, if Mr Jones buys sterling at 1.4410 and sells his dollars, he will receive £ 3 469 812.63, which can be invested at 4 % for the same period. The interest earned at the end of the period will be:

$$\frac{3\,469\,812.63 \times 92 \times 4}{365 \times 100} = \$34\,983.32$$

Thus, the total principle and interest earned at the end of the period will be £ 3 504 795.95 (£ 3 469 812.63 + £ 34 983.32).

This can then be converted back into dollars at 1.4400, which would give an amount of $ 5 046 906.17 (£ 3 504 795.95 × 1.4400). The total gain at the end of the period will be $ 21 350.61 ($ 5 046 906.17 − $ 5 025 555.56).

In a free market, however, the advantage of the higher sterling interest rate is usually neutralized by the lower value of sterling in the forward foreign exchange market and any yield pick-up will be small, or non-existent.

In calculating the forward points, users adopt a simple arithmetic formula which takes the interest rate differential per annum, converts it into a differential for the required period, and expresses the spot rate as a percentage of the differential for the period. However, it cannot be used entirely in isolation, for it assumes knowledge of relative interest rate levels by the interested party. It is, in essence, a variation on the old banking formula:

$$\text{Principle} \times \text{rate} \times \text{time} = \text{interest}$$

where the principle is the spot rate, the rate is the interest rate differential, and time is the maturity in days. Thus:

$$\frac{\text{Spot rate} \times \text{interest rate differential} \times \text{days}/360}{1 + (\text{currency interest rate} \times \text{days}/360)} = \text{pips/points}$$

In other words, the formula for dollars against currency forwards is:

$$\frac{A \times D \times (B - C)}{(100 \times E) + (C - D)}$$

which equals the number of forward points of spot currency, with 360 day basis, where:

A = spot exchange rate
B = currency interest rate
C = dollar interest rate
D = maturity in days
E = day basis

It has to be noted that, in the money market, all calculations are based on the actual number of days elapsed divided by 360, except for calculations involving sterling and some other currencies when 365 days are used. The formula is adjusted when the two currencies involved have a different day base. Also, when the value date is the last business day of a month, the corresponding date in any future month is also the last business day. For example, if the spot value date were 28 February, the value date in a one-month forward transaction would be 31 March. If the spot value date were 31 May, the 6-month forward transaction date would be 30 November. If the last day of the month is not a business day, then the value date is the next preceding business day.

8.4.1 Bids and Offers

Just as there is a bid and offer in the spot market, there is also a bid and offer rate in the forward market. This means that the forward points for both sides of the exchange rate must be quoted. A typical example of how forward rates are quoted is:

Currency	1 month	3 month
USD/JPY	19.55/19.30	62.7/61.7
USD/SFR	0.1/1.1	1.7/1.9
EUR/USD	9.07/8.99	29.5/27.8

8.4.2 To Add or to Subtract

As already mentioned, the simple rule to arrive at the forward rate is: if the forward pips decline from left to right, the currency is at a *premium* to the dollar and the forward pips are *deducted* from the spot rate. For example, if spot USD/JPY is 121.70/75, the one-month forward price is:

$$121.70 - 0.1955 \text{ and } 121.75 - 0.1930 = 121.5045/121.557$$

If the forward pips rise from left to right, the currency is at a *discount* to the dollar and the forward points are *added* to the spot. For example, if spot USD/SFR is 1.6703/08, the 3-month forward price is:

$$1.6703 + 0.00017 \text{ and } 1.6708 + 0.00019 = 1.67047/1.67099$$

The major exception is the quotation for sterling against the dollar, where if the forward pips decline from left to right, the pips are deducted but the dollar is at a premium to sterling. Occasionally, it is possible to have forward pips that have a negative number for one side of the quote and a positive number for the other. An example would be −0.7/+1.3. The rules for adding or subtracting are still the same. This type of forward pips behaviour occurs when the interest rates of the two currencies are so close that the offer side of one crosses the bid side of the other.

8.5 HOW ARE FORWARDS QUOTED?

When a market maker quotes a forward price, the trader will say:

'3-month dollar/yen 62.7 at 61.7'

where the market maker will buy and sell jpy at − 62.7 pips (sell and buy dollars) and will sell and buy Yen at − 61.7 pips (buy and sell dollars). Of course, for currencies quoted in American terms, i.e. euro, the market maker will quote a 1-month forward price as:

'1-month eur/dollar 9.07 at 8.99'

Market maker		Market maker	
Buy + sell yen	Sell + buy yen	Buy + sell dollars	Sell + buy dollars
Sell + buy dollars	Buy + sell dollars	Sell + buy eur	Buy + sell eur
−62.7	−61.7	−9.07	−8.99
Sell + Buy yen	Buy + sell yen	Sell + buy dollars	Buy + sell dollars
Buy + sell dollars	Sell + buy dollars	Buy + sell eur	Sell + buy eur
Market user		Market user	

Figure 8.1   Examples of forward quotations

where the market maker will buy and sell dollars at − 9.07 pips (sell and buy euros) and will sell and buy dollars at − 8.99 pips (buy and sell euros). Some examples of forward quotations are given in Figure 8.1.

8.6   FORWARD CROSS RATES

Forward cross rates are worked out in the same manner as for spot rates. First, calculate the forward rate from the spot rate and the forward points, then decide which currencies are being bought and sold. Finally, decide if the rates should be divided or multiplied by one another, as appropriate. For example, by using the following forward points:

	USD/JPY	USD/CHF	CHF/JPY
Spot	115.90/95	1.4382/1.4388	80.40/80.47
3-month pips	53.9–53.6	27–26	23–22

CHF/JPY 3-month forward can be worked out as:

3-month USD/JPY		3-month USD/CHF		3-month CHF/JPY	
115.90 to	115.95	1.4409 to	1.4414	80.40 to	80.47
−53.9	−53.6	−27	−26	−23	−22
115.361 to	115.414	1.4382 to	1.4388	80.17 to	80.25

Market maker

Sell yen	Buy yen
Buy dollars	Sell dollars

115.90	115.95

Buy yen	sell yen
Sell dollars	buy dollars

Market user

Market maker

Sell francs	Buy francs
Buy dollars	Sell dollars

1.4409	1.4414

Buy francs	Sell francs
Sell dollars	Buy dollars

Market user

Market maker

Sell yen	Buy yen
Buy francs	Sell francs

80.40	80.47

Buy yen	Sell yen
Sell francs	Buy francs

Market user

Figure 8.2 Calculating forward cross rates

As described previously in the sections on spot pricing and calculations, the bid for spot Swiss francs against Japanese yen is derived by taking 115.90 (bid) and dividing it by 1.4414 (offer), in order to reach the spot price of 80.40. Likewise, in order to obtain the offer spot price of Swiss francs against Japanese yen, take the offer of dollar yen, 150.95 and divide it by the bid of dollar Swiss franc 1.4382, which gives 80.47. The details are presented in Figure 8.2.

8.7 USES OF FORWARDS

Forward contracts are a common hedging product and are used by importers, exporters, investors and borrowers. They are valuable to those with existing assets or liabilities in foreign currencies and to those wanting to lock in a specific future foreign exchange rate. For example, corporations that must receive or pay foreign currencies in the future because of their normal business activities usually prefer to transfer the risk that the values of these currencies may change during the intervening period. They can use the bank forward market to establish today, the exchange rate between two currencies for a value date in the future. Generally, when corporations contract to pay to or receive from a bank foreign currency in the future, no money is exchanged until the settlement on the value date.

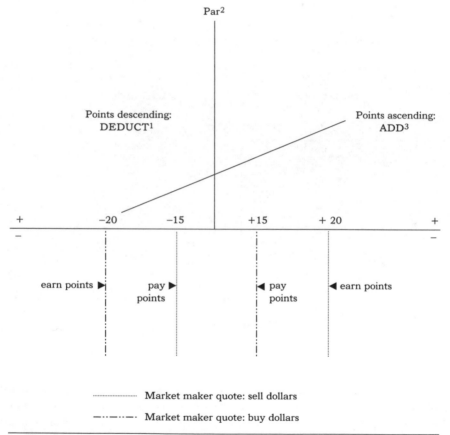

———————————— Market maker quote: sell dollars

— · · — · · — · Market maker quote: buy dollars

[1] *Deduct*: The dollar is at a discount when it is more expensive on an interest basis than the currency. These dollar discounts/currency premiums are always deducted from the spot rate.
[2] *Par*: Interest rates for both dollar and currency are equal.
[3] *Add*: The dollar is at a premium to the currency when it is cheaper on an interest basis than the currency. These dollar premiums/currency discounts are always added to the spot rate.

Figure 8.3 Example of forward transactions corporations contract to pay to or receive from a bank foreign currency in the future, no money is exchanged until the settlement on the value date

While forwards may be used to hedge payables and receivables, corporations will also hedge other assets and liabilities on a company's balance sheet. The value dates of forward contracts are often constructed to match up with the expected dates of receipts for a foreign payment, or payment of a foreign currency obligation. A forward contract can be tailored to meet a client's specific needs in terms of delivery dates and amount. In addition to transacting with clients, banks actively trade forward currency commitments among themselves.

8.7.1 Risks Involved

Because of the time span involved in forward contracts, there can be significant risks, just as on a spot deal. Credit risk, market/price risk and country risk are all potential problems. In fact, country risk is more significant than spot trades as unexpected events in a foreign country are more likely, given the longer period of exposure.

CONCLUDING REMARKS

Forwards provide certainty in the uncertain world of currency movements by locking in a specific rate, and as the forward markets are quite liquid, the bid/offer spreads are low. The interest rate differential between the dollar and another currency is expressed in points, which are fractions of that currency's exchange value against one dollar.

The forward contract is shown graphically in Figure 8.3.

9
Short- and Long-Dated Contracts

9.1 SHORT-DATED CONTRACTS

> **A short-dated contract is a foreign exchange contract that is executed today to buy one currency for another currency at a rate agreed today with settlement less than spot.**

As has been stated, most foreign exchange deals are executed for value two business days forward, or longer. However, some participants could have a need for currency the same day, the next day or the day after spot. For some currencies, like sterling and the euro, it is possible to trade for the same day value, but for the majority of currencies the earliest execution would be tomorrow.

The terminology for these differing time periods is:

Value same day : overnight (o/n)
Value tomorrow : tom next (t/n)
SPOT
Value day after : spot next (s/n)

The rates quoted for value dates occurring before spot are treated in a different way to those occurring after spot. The rules applying to a value date after spot is that if the forward pips go from high to low (20–18), they are *subtracted* from the spot rate and if the forward pips go from low to high (18–20), they are *added* to the spot rate. But, if the value date is before spot, the points are switched and the normal rule is then followed. The pips for 'overnight' and 'tom next' represent only one day each. If, therefore, a rate is calculated for value today, the pips for 'overnight' and 'tom next' have to be added together.

9.2   INTEREST RATE DIFFERENTIALS

Short dates and their equivalent rates can be more easily understood by looking at the rates over a period of time. For example, at the moment, American interest rates are higher than Japanese interest rates. As forward rates are calculated from interest rate differentials, the high interest rate currency will buy less of the low interest rate currency in order to offset the interest rate differential. Hence, the number of Japanese yen to buy one dollar will decline the further into the future one moves. Therefore, in order to conform to the interest rate structure, the short dates should be higher than spot.

If the interest rate structure was reversed, then the exchange rates would increase in time and the short dates would be worth less than spot. With any forward transaction, the quotation is based on the relationship between the prevailing interest rates of the two currencies concerned. This is shown graphically in Figure 9.1.

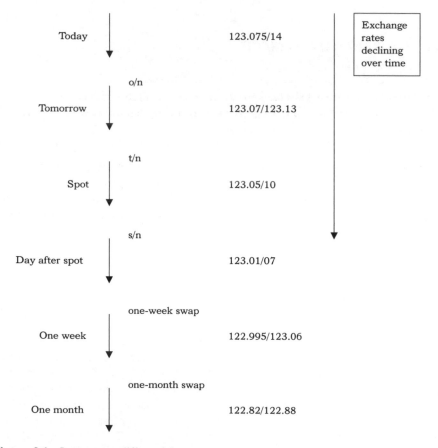

Figure 9.1   Interest rate differentials

9.3   LONG-DATED CONTRACTS

With any forward transaction, the quotation is based on the relationship between the prevailing interest rates of the two currencies concerned. However, when considering forwards beyond one year, it is necessary to account for the annual interest compounding effect.

> **A long-dated forward is one which is dealt today to buy or sell one currency at a rate agreed today with the settlement at an agreed future date, beyond one year from now.**

The short method for calculating a forward rate beyond one year is to use the normal formula for calculating forward points from interest rate differentials. However, this formula has to be modified to take into account the compounding effect of the interest.

CONCLUDING REMARKS

The principle for short- or long-dated contracts is the same as with forward rates and is made on the basis of interest rate gain or loss. The exception to the rule is that prices normally added on are deducted and prices normally deducted are added. This, actually, is not as odd as it sounds. If prices are normally quoted for spot delivery and a value tomorrow quote means the market maker will have to surrender dollars earlier than normal, there has to be some compensation.

10
Broken-Dated Contracts

A broken-dated contract is a forward contract with maturity other than the normal market quote of complete months.

10.1 CALCULATIONS

In order to price a broken-dated contract, it is necessary to interpolate between the two standard date quotations on either side of the desired maturity. For example, to work out the forward pips for the dollar against the Japanese yen for one and half months (45 days), assume the following rates:

USD/JPY spot	123.30/40
1-month forward pips	21/18
2-month forward pips	44/41

The pips for buying JPY and selling USD would be calculated according to the following:

- Work out the number of days in the period between the 1- and 2-month forward quotes, because the delivery date falls within this period. The answer is 45 days.
- Subtract the bid 1-month forward pips from the bid 2-month forward pips, which will then show what the 2-month pips are worth over the 1-month pips. The answer is 23 forward pips.
- Divide the difference in forward pips (23) by the number of days in the period between the two standard quotes (45) and multiply the answer (0.5111) by the

difference in the number of days between the required date and the last day of the 2-month quote (15). Hence, the total of those days is worth 7.7 forward pips.

• Subtract this answer (7.7) from the 2-month forward pips, giving us the forward pips for the broken date of 36.3.

The interpolated rate is the basis for the market maker's quote, but the actual rate quoted will also probably reflect the market maker's position.

10.2 OUTRIGHT FORWARDS

> **An outright forward contract is the purchase or sale of a currency for delivery on any date other than spot and not forming part of a swap operation.**

An importer might want to fix the rate today, for the delivery of a shipment in two months' time. The process for the rate on an outright is to use the spot rate and the 2-month forward pips. If the spot dollar/yen is 123.32/37 and the 2-month forward pips are 44/41, the outright price for two months' time is 122.88/96 (123.32–44 and 123.37–41). As already illustrated for a spot transaction, an outright forward transaction can be illustrated as in Figure 10.1

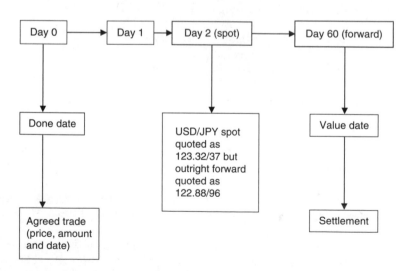

Figure 10.1 An outright forward transaction

10.3   A CONVERSATION

A conversation between the importer and the market maker could be:

Importer: What is the 2-month dollar/yen forward pips please?
Market maker: 2-month forward dollar/yen is 44 at 41
Importer: OK, spot dollar/yen in two dollars please?
Market maker: 123.32/37
Importer: At 123.32, I sell two million dollars – outright two months please.
Market maker: OK, so you sell two million dollars against the yen outright two months at an all-in rate of 122.88. Thanks. (123.32–0.44)

Notice how the importer asked for the 2-month forward pips first of all and then asked for the spot price. It is possible to ask for the spot price first of all, but because the spot price is more volatile, the market maker is unlikely to keep the spot price the same, while the forward pips are requested. Also, if the importer deals on the spot price first of all, and then requests the forward pips in order to make the deal an outright, the market maker is more likely to 'mark' the forward pips accordingly.

Glossary of Terms for Chapters 7 to 10

Below are some commonly used expressions which market makers employ. Like most esoteric enterprises, the foreign exchange market likes to surround itself with jargon and technical shorthand. Hopefully, this glossary will dispel some of the mythology.

At a discount   A currency which is less expensive to purchase forward than for spot delivery. Its interest rates are higher than those of the latter.

At a premium   A currency which is more expensive to purchase forward than for spot delivery. Its interest rates are lower than those of the latter.

Bid, wanted, firm, strong   The currency in question is appreciating, or in demand, and buyers of the currency predominate.

Broken date, odd date   A value date which is not the regular forward date and implies an odd number of days.

Cash   Same as value today, where funds are settled on the same day as the contract is struck.

End/end   If the spot value of the near end of a swap falls on the last business day of the month, the forward date must also be the last business day of the month, for example 28 February to 31 March, not 28 March.

Firm   A market maker making a commitment to a price.

For indication   Quotations which are not firm and are intended as an indication of unwillingness or inability to trade.

Forward   Any transaction, which settles on a date beyond spot. Where the maturity falls on a non-trading day, settlement takes place on the following business day.

Forward/forward   A swap price where both value dates are beyond spot.

Long, overbought   Excess of purchases over sales.

'Mine'   The trader buys the currency and amount specified at time of asking for a quote.

Offered, weak   The currency in question is depreciating and sellers of the currency predominate.

Outright   The purchase or sale of a currency for delivery for any date, other than spot not being a swap transaction.

Overnight   A swap price for today against tomorrow.

Par   Where spot is the same as the forward price, indicating that interest rates in the respective currencies are identical.

Pip   The last decimal place of a quotation.

Short dates   Usually swap prices for days up to one week.

Short, oversold   Excess of sales over purchases.

Spot date   Cash settlement two working days from the trade date. The exception to the rule is the Canadian dollar, which is one working day from the trade date.

Spot next or spot a day   A swap price for spot against the following day.

Spot rate   The price at which one currency can be bought or sold, expressed in terms of the other currency, for delivery on the spot date.

Spread   The difference between the buying and selling price of a foreign exchange quotation.

Square   Purchases and sales are equal, i.e. no position, or no further interest in dealing.

Swap (fx)   The simultaneous purchase and sale of one currency against another for two different value dates. It is the combination of a spot and a forward, or the combination of two forwards.

Swap pips, points   Used to calculate the forward price and are determined by interest rate differentials.

Tom next   A swap price for tomorrow against the next day, which is spot.

Value date, settlement date   The date agreed upon by both parties on which the two payments involved are settled.

Value tomorrow   Except in Canada, settlement is one day ahead of spot value.

'**Your risk**'   Where the response is not immediately forthcoming from a market user when a market maker has quoted a price, the market maker may, at its discretion, indicate the price is no longer firm by stating that the market user is now at risk of the price changing against him or her.

'**Yours**'   The trader sells the currency and amount specified at the time of asking for a quote.

11
Non-Deliverable Forwards

> A non-deliverable forward (NDF) is a cash settled forward and is conceptually similar to an outright forward foreign exchange transaction.

NDFs are synthetic foreign currency forward contracts on non-convertible currencies or are traded on currencies with very little liquidity in the market place. These derivatives allow corporates and other investors to hedge or take positions to local currency movements without actually dealing in the underlying.

A (notional) principle amount, forward exchange rate and forward date are all agreed at the deal's inception. The difference is that there will be no physical transfer of the principle amount in this transaction. The deal is agreed on the basis that net settlement will be made in American dollars, or another fully convertible currency, to reflect any differential between the agreed forward rate and the actual exchange rate on the agreed forward date. It is a cash-settled outright forward.

The demand for NDFs arises principally out of regulatory and liquidity issues in the underlying currency, where overseas players are essentially barred from access to the domestic market. In most cases, the local authorities actually see NDFs as a natural progression toward a free capital market.

11.1 FIXING METHODOLOGY

When a NDF deal is contracted, a fixing methodology is agreed. It specifies how a fixing spot rate is determined on the fixing date, which is normally two working days before settlement, to reflect the spot value. Generally, the fixing spot rate is based on a reference page on either Reuters or Telerate with a back up of calling between three and five market banks. Settlement is made in the major currency, paid to or by the client, and reflects the differential between the agreed upon non-deliverable forward rate and the fixing spot rate.

The NDF is quoted using foreign exchange forward market convention, with two way prices quoted as bid/offer pips, at a premium or discount to the prevailing spot market. The spreads are probably wider than would be expected in the normal forward market. As with a normal forward transaction, the market user either buys or sells the NDF, depending on the position to be hedged or according to the view of the underlying currency or interest rates.

The pitfalls of using NDFs are in part determined by how developed the domestic markets are. If NDF buyers want to unwind contracts before maturity, there may not be the liquidity for them to do so. However, as long as the underlying markets are reasonably stable, liquidity should be provided.

11.2 RISK MANAGEMENT TOOL

NDFs are a risk management tool used to hedge the risk of forward currency inconvertibility, which can result from a number of factors, including credit risk, sovereign risk, regulatory restrictions, or lack of settlement procedures. NDFs are typically utilized by banks, multinational corporates, investment managers and proprietary traders to hedge currency risk. In addition, NDFs can be used for currency arbitrage, to trade currencies where formal transaction documentation does not exist (as an off-balance-sheet product, documentation is not required) or as a tool to facilitate locking in the enhance yields of emerging market currencies. Volatile currencies can bring greater yields when compared to current short-term interest rates in America and Europe. (The characteristics of emerging markets are given in Table 11.1.)

11.3 AVAILABILITY

NDFs are available in several 'exotic' currencies, and for most NDF products prices are quoted for up to one year. It is not unusual to have the spot price being fully

Table 11.1 Characteristics of emerging markets

1. Limited currency convertibility
2. Central bank regulations
3. Illiquid markets
4. Limited hedging vehicles
5. Event/sovereign risk
6. Greater volatility
7. Cross-border risk
8. Withholding taxes

convertible, but forwards past spot being quoted only on a NDF basis. Today, most South American countries and some Far East countries operate NDFs.

11.4   EXAMPLES

To hedge against a currency depreciation when the fixing rate is greater than the outright price at maturity, the purchaser of the NDF would receive from the seller the difference between the fixing rate and the outright rate in cash terms. This amount can be calculated by using the following formula:

$$\frac{(F - O) \times N}{F}$$

where

$F =$ fixing rate
$O =$ outright price
$N =$ notional amount

Obviously, if the fixing rate is less than the outright price at maturity, the opposite will apply.

To hedge against a currency appreciation where the fixing rate is greater than the outright price at maturity, the seller of the NDF pays the buyer the difference between the fixing rate and the outright rate in cash terms, calculated as above. As with a purchase, if the fixing rate is less than the outright price, the opposite will apply. An example of the above would be:

Notional amount:	$ 10 000 000
Maturity:	90 days
Spot:	2.0000 fx/$
90-day NDF:	0.0100
Outright:	2.0100 fx/$
Fixing rate:	2.0200 fx/$

At maturity, the purchaser of the NDF will receive from the seller:

$$\frac{(2.0200 - 2.0100) \times 10\,000\,000}{2.0200} = \frac{0.0100 \times 10\,000\,000}{2.0200} = \$\,49\,504.95$$

Another example is where, say, an investor has invested $ 2 000 000 in stock on the Korean stock market for one year. The investor expects the stock market to rise, but is worried about potential Korean won (Krw) depreciation. The investor wishes to hedge the foreign exchange exposure using an NDF. A non-deliverable forward rate of Krw 1310 per dollar is agreed between the bank and the client. The principle amount is $ 2 000 000. There are three possible outcomes in one year's time:

- the Krw has reached the forward rate;
- depreciated further;
- appreciated relative to the forward rate.

The following shows examples of the three scenarios:

	Outcome A	*Outcome B*	*Outcome C*
USD/KRW	Depreciated	–	Appreciated
Fixing spot rate	1330	1310	1290
Equivalent amount	$ 1 969 925	$ 2 000 000	$ 2 031 008
Settlement	Bank pays client $ 30 075	No net payment	Client pays $ 31 008

In all outcomes, the client has achieved the objective of hedging the KRW exposure at 1310.

- In outcome A, the exchange rate loss that the client would suffer if the investor sells the investment and exchange the Krw proceeds in the spot market, is compensated by the proceeds of the NDF.
- In outcome C, the client's exchange gain on realization of the investment is countered by the payment the investor makes on the NDF.

For a corporate, an example would be where the corporate is due to receive Philippine pesos (Php) 102 000 000 in three months' time. They are concerned about potential depreciation and wish to hedge this exposure using an NDF. Assume the agreed non-deliverable forward rate is Php 51 per dollar. The principle amount of Php 102 000 000 is equivalent to $ 2 000 000. Again, there are three possible outcomes in three months' time:

	Outcome A	*Outcome B*	*Outcome C*
PHP/USD	Depreciated	–	Appreciated
Fixing spot rate	51.5	51.0	50.5
Equivalent amount	$ 1 980 583	$ 2 000 000	$ 2 019 802
Settlement	Bank pays client $ 19 417	No net payment	Client pays bank $ 19 802

The consequences are as in the above example.

Please note: All rates and other figures are for illustrative purposes only.

11.5   TYPICAL RISKS ENCOUNTERED

- **Contingent risk** – This exists when the dollar value of anticipated but not yet committed cash flows is subject to changes in exchange rates (see Figures 11.1 and 11.2).
- **Sovereign risk** – This is the risk that the Government of a country may interfere with the repayment of a debt. For example, a borrower in a foreign country may be economically sound and capable of repaying a loan in local currency. However, his country's government may not permit him to repay a loan to a foreign bank because of a lack of foreign exchange or for political reasons. The bank making the loan in the first place must take this sovereign risk into account and reflect it in the interest rate.
- **Transaction exposure** – This arises whenever any company unit commits to pay or receive funds in a currency other than its national currency.
- **Translation exposure** – This is the risk that financial statements of overseas subsidiaries of a company will gain or lose value because of exchange rate movements when translated into the currency of the parent company upon consolidation.

11.6   THE CURRENCIES OF EMERGING MARKETS

The following are examples of some of the better-known currencies, which are non-deliverable today.

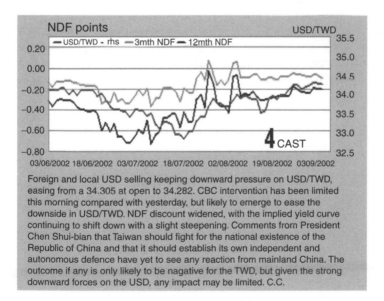

Figure 11.1 USD/TWD downward pressure widening NDF discount. Reproduced by permission of 4CAST Limited. *Source:* 4castweb.com

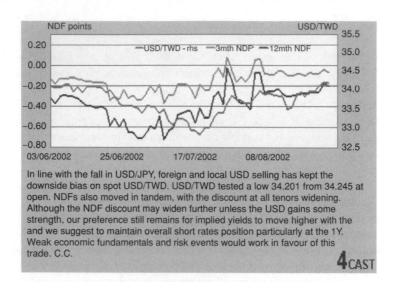

Figure 11.2 USD/JPY dragging spot USD/TWD and NDFs lower. Reproduced by permission of 4CAST Limited. *Source*: 4castweb.com

| China | The People's Bank of China (PBOC) is China's central bank and the Government institution responsible for formulating and implementing monetary policy. Unlike other countries where the central bank will set an individual base rate, the PBOC will make changes that apply to a large array of lending and deposit rates. The PBOC maintains the renminbi (or yuan) in a managed float, where the currency is no longer pegged to the US dollar, but managed with reference to a basket of currencies. |

China The People's Bank of China (PBOC) is China's central bank and the Government institution responsible for formulating and implementing monetary policy. Unlike other countries where the central bank will set an individual base rate, the PBOC will make changes that apply to a large array of lending and deposit rates. The PBOC maintains the renminbi (or yuan) in a managed float, where the currency is no longer pegged to the US dollar, but managed with reference to a basket of currencies.

Korea The Ministry of Finance and Economy principally determines foreign exchange policy while the central bank, the Bank of Korea (BOK) controls exchange movements according to this policy. According to the Bank of Korea Act, maintaining price stability is the primary objective of BOK monetary policy. Despite recent liberalization, offshore access to spot and forward markets is still limited.

Philippines The Central Bank of the Philippines (BSP), is responsible for formulating and implementing monetary policy and foreign exchange controls. Since 1992, the BSP has maintained a free float currency regime where the value of the peso is determined by market forces. However, the BSP will intervene in the market to defend against what it considers to be speculative movements in the currency.

Taiwan	The Central Bank of China (CBC) is the organization responsible for establishing Taiwan's monetary policy. At present, the Taiwan dollar is a managed float currency with the CBC regularly intervening to smooth volatility.
Indonesia	The Central Bank of the Republic of Indonesia's main responsibility is to maintain stability in the financial system and in the rupiah for long-term sustainable development. As Indonesia uses a managed float currency regime, Bank Indonesia (BI) can intervene in the foreign exchange market to smooth any volatility. Since the Asian crisis in the late 1990s, the rupiah has been volatile and political uncertainty has kept trading volume low in the spot market.
Argentina	Argentina experienced a major economic crisis in 2001/2002, resulting in the country defaulting on its debt obligations. As a result, Argentina abandoned their currency board convertibility system (established 1991) which consisted in pegging the peso to the American dollar at a rate of 1-to-1. Argentina now follows a managed floating regime, with heavy interventions from the Banco Central de la Republica Argentina (BCRA) in order to prevent the peso from strengthening in real terms.
Brazil	Monetary policy is the responsibility of Banco Central do Brasil (BCB) as well as the Ministry of Finance and the National Monetary Council. The BCB acts as the superintendent of the currency and maintains the right to intervene in the currency market during periods of excess volatility. The Brazilian real floats freely against the dollar after the January 1999 devaluation. However, it remains restricted to offshore counterparties.
Chile	The Chilean peso has been a floating currency since 1999, when the Central Bank, Banco Central de Chile (BCC) discontinued the use of an exchange rate target band. The BCC sets monetary policy by announcing its benchmark inerts rates and by managing liquidity in the market via a combination of open market operations, repo operations and lines of credit and deposits. The BCC does occasionally intervene in the currency market, normally to add liquidity and dampen volatility.
Colombia	The Colombian Central Bank, Banco de la Republica, implemented a managed float currency regime in September 1999. It maintains the right to intervene in the currency, which is generally done through options transactions to mitigate both excessive strength and weakness in the peso. If the currency moves more than 5 % in either direction on any given day, the central bank may intervene aggressively to smoothen volatility in the peso. The peso NDF market is among the smaller of the Latam region.

Peru   The Central Reserve Bank of Peru, the Banco Central de Reserva
                      del Peru (BCRP) was established to implement monetary policy in
                      Peru. Currently, the BCRP maintains a managed float currency
                      regime. Although the sol floats freely, the bank will intervene to
                      smooth excess volatility. Intervention is not, however, conducted on
                      a regular basis. This NDF market is very thin with limited liquidity
                      and participants.

11.7   INDEX-LINKED DEPOSITS

An index-linked deposit is basically a restructured NDF. It is a deposit held in a
major currency with its return linked to the exchange rate of an NDF and earning an
enhanced coupon. The coupon reflects the implied local interest rates derived from
the NDF market, which may be significantly higher than the major currency interest
rates. The index-linked deposit is particularly suitable for asset managers who need
to hold a physical asset, but at the same time wish to gain access and exposure to
higher yielding markets.

Index-linked deposits are available in two types, namely those linked to principal
and interest and those purely linked to principal. The former offers a higher coupon
but exposes both principal and interest to exchange rate fluctuations; whereas the
latter exposes only the principal. Both types of deposit are not principal protected.
These deposits not only have many of the same advantages as NDFs, but they also
often allow depositors to assume a lower credit risk or to earn more interest than
depositing onshore. Moreover, they can be used as a form of collateral for NDFs.

CONCLUDING REMARKS

An NDF is a short-term committed forward 'cash settlement' currency derivative
instrument. It is essentially an outright (forward) foreign exchange contract whereby,
on the contracted settlement date, profit or loss is adjusted between the two counterparties based on the difference between the contracted NDF rate and the prevailing
spot foreign exchange rates on an agreed notional amount.

The NDF rate is the rate agreed between the two counterparties on the transaction
date. This is essentially the outright (or forward) rate of the currencies dealt. The
notional amount is the 'face value' of the NDF, which is agreed between the two
counterparties. It should again be noted that there is never any intention to exchange
both currencies' principal sums – the only movement is the difference between the
NDF rate and the prevailing spot market rate, and this amount is settled on the
settlement date.

Every NDF has a fixing date and a settlement (delivery) date. The fixing date is
the day and time whereby the comparison between the NDF rate and the prevailing

spot rate is made. The settlement date is the day whereby the difference is paid or received.

As it is a 'cash settlement' instrument, there is no movement of the principal amounts of the two currencies contracted. The only movement is the settlement amount representing the difference between the contracted NDF rates and prevailing spot rate. Hence, NDFs are 'noncash' products, which are off the balance sheet and as the principal sums do not move, possess very much lower counterparty risks.

NDFs are committed short-term instruments. Both the counterparties are committed and are obliged to honour the deal. Of course, the user can cancel an existing contract by entering into another offsetting deal at the prevailing market rate.

The more active banks will quote NDFs between one month and one year, although some will quote up to two years on request. Odd-dated NDFs can also be requested.

It should also be noted, that NDFs are quoted with the dollar as the reference currency – that is, they are quoted in terms of dollar against other third currencies and the settlement is also in dollars.

Without an NDF, an investor who wanted to take advantage of the type of enhanced yields available in the emerging markets would have to do the following:

- Buy the spot currency and sell dollars.
- Invest in a local risk-free asset (i.e. government bond).
- Fund the dollars at Libor. (At maturity, the investor receives the capital plus interest.)
- Sell the currency on the spot market and purchase dollars.

As to the future for NDFs, great strides are already being taken to open up these markets. For example, non-deliverable forwards on seven Asian currencies are now available on an electronic platform owned by one of the premier interdealer brokers. Pricing is available for one month's duration and are in Chinese renminbi (CNY), Korean won (KRW), Indian rupee (INR), Indonesian rupiah (IDR), Malaysian ringgit (MYR), Philippine peso (PHP) and Taiwan dollar (TWD). As the NDF markets continue to develop and become more commoditized, the market will increasingly benefit from an electronic trading solution. The NDF market is maturing but, at the end of the day, it will be up to the individual monetary authorities as to whether or not their currency becomes fully convertible.

12
Foreign Exchange Swaps

A foreign exchange swap is the simultaneous purchase and sale of one currency against another for two different value dates. One of the value dates is usually the spot date and the other is a date in the future. In a typical swap transaction, one currency amount is held constant for both dates of the transaction. Most foreign exchange swaps have a maturity of less than one year.

> A forward/forward is a swap where both the near date and the end date are forward dates.

In fact, a swap may be most easily understood as simply the **combination** of a spot and a forward, or the combination of two forwards. It can be the combination of a purchase with a simultaneous forward sale or a sale with a simultaneous forward purchase. Like forward contracts, swaps are regularly for periods of one, two, three, six and 12 months from the spot value date. Frequently, however, the date is customized to meet a client's needs.

Forward contract prices are determined, as before, by the current spot price between the two currencies and the interest rates prevailing in each of the two countries. For example, a company could sell dollars and buy Swiss francs spot, and buy dollars and sell Swiss francs three months forward. The cash flows in such an exercise is similar to borrowing one currency (Swiss francs) and investing in another (dollars). The exposure to the company is one of interest rate risk rather than currency risk. Consequently, a bank will only charge, or pay, the interest differential.

12.1 THE VALUE OF FOREIGN EXCHANGE SWAPS

Swaps are used primarily by investors and borrowers, and for cash management purposes. They are valuable to those who have liquidity in one currency but need liquidity in another currency. Typically, a client will buy spot and sell forward to generate liquidity in the currency purchased at spot. That is, if a client exchanges dollars for francs at spot and simultaneously exchanges francs forward for dollars, the client has created liquidity in francs (i.e. has them to spend) until the forward date. A foreign exchange swap is an alternative to straight borrowing in a foreign currency.

A swap allows the two parties involved to use a currency for a period in exchange for another currency not needed at that time. For example, companies can access foreign currency to finance foreign currency denominated assets, such as those of a foreign subsidiary. Hence, foreign exchange swaps can help clients to diversify their investments, to fund intracompany loans, to fund a position rather than use the money markets, to potentially improve the yield with no exchange risk in conjunction with a foreign currency investment, and to minimize borrowing costs in certain cases by using a swap rather than straight borrowing in a foreign currency.

In such a contract, the exposure is therefore one of interest rate risk rather than currency risk. Consequently, market makers will only charge, or pay, the interest differential. In the swap market, this interest differential is expressed, again, in points or pips.

12.2   CALCULATIONS

The formula for determining the interest rate differential underlying the swap pips is:

$$C - \left(\frac{36\,000}{T} + C \right) \frac{S}{B} = 360/360 \text{ arbitrage}$$

where

C = currency interest rate
T = period in number of days
S = swap pips as a decimal added or deducted
B = outright forward rate.

Swap pips are unequal, which can be seen in Figure 12.1.

As can be seen, the client has to borrow dollars at the higher rate, but can only invest yen at the lower rate. Similarly, the client has to borrow yen at a rate lower than the deposit rate in dollars.

Consider the following quotation:

Spot USD/SFR	1.4791	1.4796
3-month forward points	25.5	24.5
3-month dollar deposit	1.72 %	1.82 %
3-month Swiss franc deposit	1.09 %	1.17 %

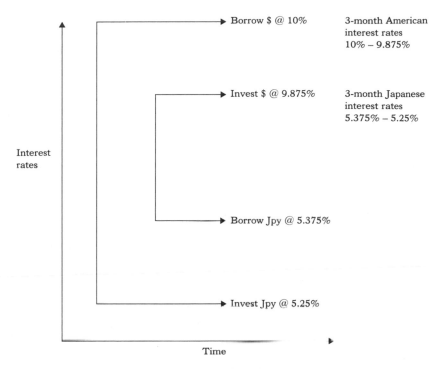

Figure 12.1 Example of unequal swap pips

In order to choose the number of points to be applied in the swap, analyse the cash at maturity. In the above example, the company is buying dollars and selling Swiss francs, which is the right-hand side of a foreign exchange quote, so the number of points is 24.5. The number of points represents the interest differential when borrowing Swiss francs and investing dollars. Similarly, 25.5 points represents the interest differential when borrowing dollars and investing Swiss francs.

12.2.1 Points of Note

There are two points to note about foreign exchange swaps.

- Firstly, as the swap pips determine the price of the swap, the spot rate used is less important. In practice, market makers tend to use the middle rate when actually processing the swap transaction. The key point to note is that whichever spot rate is chosen, the forward rate is determined by adjusting that spot rate by the swap pips.
- Secondly, the amount of one currency in a swap is kept constant. Typically, this is the dollar, thus the same amount of dollars is sold and bought in the transaction.

12.3 USES OF FOREIGN EXCHANGE SWAPS

As mentioned above, swaps are undertaken together with a money market operation to take advantage of imperfect exchange rate and interest rate differentials. This is particularly of use to companies, which have a borrowing advantage in one currency or type of facility over another, i.e. acceptance facility.

Swaps are also used where the domestic money market may not offer the necessary investment possibilities. For example, the smaller Swiss companies and wealthy private clients place short-term Swiss franc deposits with the Swiss banks domestically. Since there is a shortage of domestic money market instruments in which to invest these deposits, the Swiss banks may place them abroad, mainly in dollars, through swaps.

Finally, a swap can be used to hedge exposure. For example, a client wishes to buy Japanese yen against dollars three months forward. The bank can cover the obligation to provide the Japanese yen by purchasing them spot and undertaking a 3-month dollar against Japanese yen swap, giving up the use of Japanese yen, but getting the use of dollars for the period. At maturity, the bank uses the Japanese yen received under the swap to meet the obligation to the client, and the dollars received from the client to meet the dollar obligation under the swap.

Alternatively, a client can use a swap to roll a hedge forward. For example, the client may have entered into a contract to buy Swiss francs against dollars forward. If, in three months' time, the dollars do not materialize, the hedge would be extended. This can be achieved using a swap, whereby the original forward is closed out by the spot transaction and the exposure is covered by the forward transaction.

CONCLUDING REMARKS

Swap risks are almost identical to those for forwards. A swap effectively becomes a forward once the near date has settled. The difference between a forward and a swap is that to do a swap there must be two transactions in opposite directions at different times.

13
Currency Swaps

A currency swap is an agreement between two counterparties to exchange future cash flows. There are two fundamental types: the cross-currency swap and the interest rate (single-currency) swap.

> A cross-currency swap involves the exchange of cash flows in one currency for those in another with an agreement to reverse that transaction at a future date.
>
> An interest rate swap changes the basis on which income streams or liabilities are received or paid on a specified principal amount.

From a foreign exchange point of view, cross-currency swaps are much more relevant as they allow companies to borrow in the most efficient market, usually one in which the company have not borrowed too heavily in the past. The major difference between cross-currency swaps and currency forwards is that there is only one contract in the case of swaps, whereas forwards require separate contracts for each payment of interest and principal.

Figure 13.1 presents, in graphic form, the three stages of a currency swap.

13.1   TECHNIQUE INVOLVED

> Currency forwards involve amounts of two currencies being exchanged for an agreed period of time and re-exchanged at maturity at the same exchange rate.

An interest rate swap is exclusively concerned with the exchange of cash flows relating to the interest payments on the designated notional amount. However, there is no exchange of notional amount at the inception of the contract. The notional

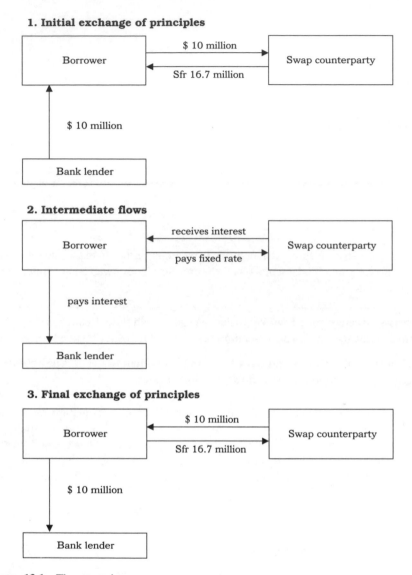

Figure 13.1   The stages in a currency swap

amount is the same for both sides of the currency and it is delineated in the same currency, i.e. principle exchange is redundant.

In the case of a currency swap, however, principle exchange is not redundant. The exchange of principle on the notional amounts is done at market rates, often using the same rate for the transfer at inception as is employed at maturity.

For example, consider an American-based company that has raised money by issuing a Swiss franc-denominated Eurobond with fixed semi-annual coupon payments of 6 % on 100 million Swiss francs. Up front, the company receives 100 million Swiss francs from the proceeds of the Eurobond issue. In essence, they are using the Swiss francs to fund their American operations.

Because this issue is funding American-based operations, the company is going to have to convert the 100 million Swiss francs into dollars. This can be done by entering into a currency swap whereby the Swiss franc debt can be converted into a dollar like debt.

The American company can agree to exchange the 100 million Swiss francs at inception into dollars, receive the Swiss franc coupon payments on the same dates as the coupon payments are due to the company's Eurobond investors: pay dollar coupon payments tied to a preset index and re-exchange the dollar notional into Swiss francs at maturity.

13.2   INTEREST PAYABLE

Thus lies the fundamental difference between a currency swap and the classic foreign exchange swap. During the life of the currency swap, each currency bears an agreed rate of interest, which is usually paid or received at intervals. Under a foreign exchange swap, no interest is payable on either currency. Rather, the price at which the currencies will be exchanged at maturity takes account of the interest differential between the two.

Thus, if sterling rates for one year are at 5 % and the dollar rates are at 2 %, the theoretical forward exchange rate between the two currencies is 3 % less than the spot rate prevailing. Under a one-year currency swap between the two, the rate for the re-exchange at the end of one year will be the same as that used at the start, but interest will be payable or receivable on each currency. In the simple case of a one-year swap between two currencies at a fixed rate of interest, the two techniques are little different. Consider, however, a five-year traditional foreign exchange swap between dollars and Swiss francs. The forward foreign exchange rate will represent the compounded interest rate differential between the two currencies and only two cash flows will occur, namely the spot transaction and the forward leg in five years, at a radically different exchange rate.

Under a currency swap between dollars and Swiss francs for five years, an amount of each currency would be exchanged at the start (determined by the spot rate prevailing), the party receiving the francs would pay an agreed interest rate periodically, as would the party receiving the dollars. At the end of five years, the same amount of each currency would be re-exchanged. There is no need for the rate of interest applicable to each currency to be on a fixed basis, it can be a floating rate tied to Libor, for example. Indeed, the vast majority of currency swaps currently transacted are between dollars at 6-month Libor and another currency at a fixed rate of interest, payable either bi-annually or annually as agreed between the two parties.

13.3 BENEFITS OF CURRENCY SWAPS

13.3.1 Flexibility

Currency swaps give companies extra flexibility to exploit their comparative advantage in their respective borrowing markets. Also, currency swaps allow companies to exploit advantages across a matrix of currencies and maturities.

CONCLUDING REMARKS

The currency swap market has become a liquid and cost-effective market for corporate treasurers to achieve long-term currency hedges for their liabilities. Today, one of the most common transactions in the currency swap market is that related to a capital market debt issue, which is then swapped in its entirety to another currency that the borrower requires. Also, an interesting application of the currency swap has been to generate foreign exchange prices by combining two or more 'zero-coupon' swaps against floating rate dollars, which cancel out the floating rate flows and leave one with an exchange of a given amount of one currency against another at a future date, which is precisely similar to a long-term foreign exchange transaction. Under a zero-coupon swap, the fixed rate interest payable/receivable is not paid until maturity and is compounded at the same time as it is paid.

Because of the exchange and re-exchange of notional principle amounts, the currency swap generates a larger credit exposure than an interest rate swap.

14
Foreign Exchange Options

The currency options market shares its origins with the new markets in derivative products, which have blossomed in recent years. They were developed to cope with the rise in volatility in the financial markets world wide. In the foreign exchange markets, the dramatic rise (1983–1985) and the subsequent fall (1985–1987) in the dollar caused major problems for central banks, corporate treasurers, and international investors alike. Windfall foreign exchange losses became enormous for the treasurer who failed to hedge, or who hedged too soon, or who borrowed money in the wrong currency. The investors in the international bond market soon discovered that the risk on their bond positions could appear insignificant relative to their currency exposure. Therefore, currency options were developed, not as another interesting off-balance-sheet trading vehicle but as an alternative risk management tool to the spot and forward foreign exchange markets. They are a product of currency market volatility and owe their existence to the demands of foreign exchange users for alternative hedging and exposure management techniques.

14.1 DEFINITIONS

> **A foreign exchange option gives the holder the right, but not the obligation, to buy or sell a certain currency against another, at a certain rate and at/by a certain date in the future.**

The most important factor of an option, in comparison to a foreign exchange transaction, is that the buyer has the right, but not the obligation, to buy or sell a specified quantity of a currency at a specified rate on or before a specified date. For this right, the buyer pays a premium to the seller or writer of the currency option, usually at the outset. For currency options, the premium is often expressed as a percentage of the notional amount covered. The essential characteristics of a currency option for its owner are those of risk limitation and unlimited profit potential. It is similar to an insurance policy. Instead of an individual paying a premium and insuring a house against fire risk, a company pays a premium to insure itself against adverse foreign exchange risk movements. This premium is the buyer's maximum cost.

The terms used in the options market can be confusing, but the principle terms or jargon used can be summarized as follows:

- The option buyer is called the **buyer** and the option seller the **writer**.
- A **call** gives the buyer the right to buy a specific quantity of a currency at an agreed rate over a given period.
- A **put** gives the buyer the right to sell a specific quantity of a currency at an agreed rate over a given period.
- The **premium** is the price paid for the option. With a currency option this can be expressed in different ways and is usually paid with spot value from the initial deal date.
- The **principle amount** is the amount of currency which the buyer can buy or sell.
- **Exercise** is the process by which the option is converted into an underlying foreign exchange contract.
- The **strike price** or **exercise rate** is the exchange rate at which the option may be exercised.
- **Expiry date** is the final date on which the option may be exercised.
- A **European** style option can be exercised at any time but the funds will be transferred on the maturity date. In practice, most European style options are not exercised until the expiry date.
- An **American** style option can be exercised at any time up to and including the expiry date with the funds being transferred with spot value from exercise.

It is important to note that, due to the nature of foreign exchange, all currency options are a put on one currency and a call on another. For example, a dollar call/Swiss franc put gives the buyer the right to buy dollars and the right to sell Swiss francs.

14.2   EXCHANGE VS OVER-THE-COUNTER OPTIONS

Foreign exchange options can be traded on an exchange or in the over-the-counter (OTC) market, i.e. between two parties. Exchange-traded options are standardized contracts with fixed maturity dates, strike prices and contract sizes, although each exchange has its own contract specifications and trading rules. OTC option specifications are much more flexible as maturity, strike price amount, etc., can be negotiated before dealing.

Exchange-traded options can be characterized by as follows:

- Currencies are quoted mainly against dollars although recently some crosses have become available.
- Strike prices are at fixed intervals and quoted in dollars or cents per unit(s) of currency.
- Contract sizes are fixed.
- Fixed expiry dates, generally at three-month intervals, e.g. delivery on the third-Wednesday of March, June, September and December.
- Premium is paid up front and on the same day as the transaction.
- Options are usually American style.

One major advantage of standardized contracts is that the exchange acts as the counterparty to each trade. Credit risk (the risk of the writer defaulting on the option) is therefore minimized and anonymity between counterparties can be preserved. It should be noted that currency options on the Chicago Mercantile Exchange (CME) are options on futures rather than options on the spot currency. Hence, if a call is exercised, the buyer receives a long futures position rather than a spot position, and the opposite applies to the buyer of a put.

Over-the-counter options have the following characteristics:

- Strike rates, contract sizes and maturity are all subject to negotiation. An institution can structure its own option requirements, enabling it, for example, to make cross rate transactions.
- Maturities can run from several hours to five years.
- The buyer has the direct credit risk on the writer.
- Only the counterparties directly involved know the price at which the option is dealt.
- The premium is normally paid with spot value from the transaction date with delivery of the underlying instrument also typically with spot value from expiry.
- Options style can be American or European, but the majority are European.

For example, Bank A buys from Bank B a 1.5700 European style sterling call/dollar put on £ 10 million, with a maturity of six months. Bank A buys the option through the OTC market for a premium of $ 0.02 per £ 1 principle. In this example:

Buyer:	Bank A
Writer (seller):	Bank B
Strike price:	1.5700
Principle amount:	£ 10 000 000
Expiry date:	6 months
Premium:	$ 200 000 (£ 10 m × $ 0.02)

14.3   APPLICATION OF FOREIGN EXCHANGE OPTIONS

The users of the option market are widespread and varied, but the main users are organizations whose business involves foreign exchange risk. Options may be a suitable means of removing that risk and are an alternative to forward foreign exchange transactions. In general, the exchange-traded options markets will be accessed by the professional market makers and currency risk managers. The standardization of options contracts promotes tradability, but this is at the expense of flexibility.

In spite of the fact that options are becoming more and more popular with corporate clients, funds and private individuals, there is still some client resistance to using options to manage currency exposures. Some clients consider options to be expensive and/or speculative. When you buy an option, the most you can lose is the premium (price paid for the option). In some cases, options can help to minimize downside risk, while allowing participation in the upside potential. One of the reasons that clients may choose to use an option instead of a forward to manage their downside risk, is this opportunity to participate in the upside profit potential which is given up with a forward contract. Clients who buy currency options enjoy protection from any unfavourable exchange rate movements. (This is shown graphically in Figure 14.1.)

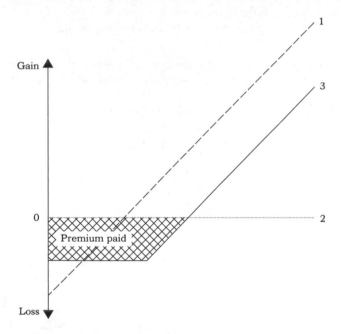

1. Do nothing: potential loss or gain
2. Forward forex contract: no potential loss or gain
3. Purchase an option – loss limited to premium paid
   while retaining upside potential

Figure 14.1   Foreign exchange considerations

Companies use currency options to hedge contingent/economic exposures, to hedge an existing currency exposure, and possibly to profit from currency fluctuations, while funds may use options to enhance yield.

A simplified decision tree on when to use options, or the various other products available, can be quite useful. The decision-making process assumes a firm view of likely future rate movements, as indecisiveness can only be accommodated by the use of currency options, which can be an expensive solution for many hedging requirements. The more confident the forecast, the simpler the products needed to satisfy needs. The simpler the product, the cheaper the cost. If the forecast is confident that rates will be favourable, then it is best to stay unhedged or to take out an option with the full confidence that the premium cost will be recovered, as the option means that any unexpected downturn will be catered for. Similarly, if no change is expected, then the position should be covered with the cheapest hedge possible. A confident forecast that rates will be unfavourable would call for a forward contract. An example of an exposure management decision tree is shown as in Figure 14.2.

Sometimes a strategy may involve more than one option and some option strategies employ multiple and complex combinations. Certain combinations can yield a low or no-cost option strategy by trading off the premium spent on buying an option with the premium earned by selling an option.

Hence, the purchase of a currency option may help by limiting the downside currency fluctuation risk while retaining the upside potential, by providing unlimited potential for gain, by providing a hedge for a contingent risk, and by enabling

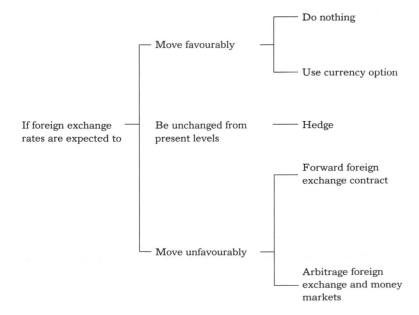

Figure 14.2 Exposure management decision tree

planning with more certainty. On the other hand, selling a currency option may assist in providing immediate income from premium received and provides flexibility when used with other tools as part of an exchange rate strategy.

In general, the applications of foreign exchange options can be summarized as follows.

- To cover foreign exchange exposure:
  - on existing exposure;
  - on contingent exposure;
  - against a budget rate;
  - as disaster insurance.
- To speculate:
  - on the direction of spot;
  - on a volatile or quiet market;
  - on the timing of spot movement;
  - on changing interest rate differentials.
- To lock in profit:
  - as an investment:
    in a speculative asset; *or*
    to alleviate loan costs; *or*
    to improve deposit yields;
  - as a funding tool:
    to generate a cash flow (short position); *or*
    to transfer cash to another entity;
  - as a tax management tool:
    to transfer profit and loss over time.

For a hedger, in terms of exchange rate risk management, currency options can be used to guarantee a budget rate for a transaction. By purchasing a call (the right to buy) the maximum cost can be fixed for a purchase and by purchasing a put (the right to sell) the minimum size of a receipt can be fixed. The purchase of the option involves paying a premium but gives the buyer the full protection against unfavourable moves while retaining full potential to profit should rates subsequently move beneficially. This contrasts with a forward contract, which locks the hedger into a fixed exchange rate, where no premium is payable but no benefit can be taken from subsequent favourable moves.

In the case of trading, to assume risk in order to make a profit, traders use options to benefit from both directional views and/or changes in volatility. (This allows profit to be made from the expectation that volatility will either increase or decrease over a period of time.) For example, in order to take a directional view, an options trader might feel strongly that the dollar will strengthen against the Swiss franc in the next three months from its current level of $/Sfr 1.66. The trader buys a dollar call (right to buy), Swiss franc put (right to sell) option with a strike price of 1.6835, with expiry in three months' time.

The trader has two choices: to hold the option to expiry, and if the spot rate has risen to, for example, $/Sfr 1.73, the trader would exercise his right to buy dollars and sell Swiss francs at 1.6835, and hence, make money. If the spot rate is below $/Sfr 1.6835 at expiry, then the maximum loss is limited to the premium paid for the option. Alternatively, if the spot rate rises, say one month after the trader has purchased the option, the trader could choose to sell the option back. By doing this, the trader will recoup both the time value and intrinsic value of the option.

14.4 ALTERNATIVES TO FOREIGN EXCHANGE OPTIONS

Quite often there really seems to be little point in paying a premium for an option when a foreign exchange forward would suffice, but the benefits of an option really do have to be considered. Hence, the difference between an OTC foreign exchange option and foreign exchange forward can be seen in Table 14.1, and the differences between buying an OTC foreign exchange option and leaving the position unhedged, i.e. leaving the position open, can be seen in Table 14.2.

Table 14.1 Forex options versus forex forwards

Options	Forwards
Right but not the obligation to buy or sell a currency	Obligation to buy or sell a currency
Premium payable	No premium payable
Wide range of strike prices	Only one forward rate for a particular date
Retains unlimited profit potential while limiting downside risk	Eliminates the upside potential as well as the downside risk
Flexible delivery date of currency (can buy an option for a longer period than necessary)	Fixed delivery date of currency

Table 14.2 Forex options versus forex open positions

Option	Open position
Right but no obligation to buy or sell a currency	No obligation to buy or sell a currency
Premium payable	No premium payable
Retains unlimited profit potential while limiting downside risk	Profit and loss potential unlimited
Flexible delivery date of currency (can buy an option for a longer period than needed)	Indefinite delivery date of currency

	Financial risk	Profit potential	Credit risk
Option buyer	Limited to premium paid	Unlimited	Credit worthiness of option seller
Option seller (writer)	Unlimited	Limited to premium earned	Settlement risk if option is exercised

Figure 14.3   Risk profile of option buyer/seller

14.5   PARTIES AND THE RISKS INVOLVED

Two parties are involved in foreign exchange options: the option buyer and the option seller (writer), and Figure 14.3 outlines a risk profile for each. The option buyer has the right to demand fulfilment of the option contract. The owner can exercise the option. The option buyer pays a premium for that right. The option seller (writer) grants the right and receives a premium for accepting the obligation to fulfil the option contract, if the buyer demands.

As in spot and forward foreign exchange contracts, there are risks involved in currency options. If the option expires worthless (i.e. is not exercised), then there is no real credit risk.

If it is exercised, there is transaction-related risk that is similar to the risk on a spot settlement. Because an option buyer enjoys the dual benefits of insurance and upside potential, the option seller/writer is subject to a greater degree of market/price risk than when it enters into a forward contract. As for country risk, it is similar to that for forwards and swaps.

14.6   USERS OF FOREIGN EXCHANGE OPTIONS

As Figure 14.3 shows, there is one very important factor to remember regarding currency options: for the buyer of an option, the maximum risk is limited to the premium paid, but for the option seller, the maximum profit is limited to the premium received and the seller is potentially exposed to unlimited losses. Additionally, because of the credit risk involved when writing options, there are typically fewer restrictions on those wishing to buy options than on those wishing to sell.

Writing options on exchanges tends to be simpler as the credit risks are controlled by a margin system. The margin is a small percentage of the value of the contract, which must be deposited to cover losses up to a certain limit. The margin is usually adjusted on each trading day and, on occasions, more frequently to take account of market movements. However, the greater flexibility available in the OTC market allows some of the credit difficulties to be pursued and overcome. Participants in the foreign exchange currency options market include:

- *Banks* – who provide a service for their clients, to manage their own foreign exchange risk, and in order to take a directional and/or volatility view.
- *Supranationals and sovereigns* – all issuers of debt in foreign currencies will have exchange rate exposure, which must be managed.
- *Multinational companies* – multinationals and their subsidiaries will have funds and crossborder transactions in several currencies and so will be subject to foreign exchange risk.
- *Importers and exporters* – any company that imports or exports goods to a foreign country will have exposure to fluctuations in exchange rates.
- *Investors in foreign currency securities* – investors in foreign securities will be exposed to fluctuations in the currency in which the securities are denominated.
- *High net worth individuals* – such individuals may use exchange-traded currency options for speculation on exchange rates because of the gearing they offer.

For example, a British-based company exports consumer goods to several countries. Currently, the company has contracted to supply 10 million dollars worth of goods to America and expects to receive payment in three months' time, in dollars. The company believes that the dollar will appreciate against sterling over the next three months.

There are several alternative strategies. The company can:

(1) leave the future cash flow unhedged in the belief that the exchange rate will move in their favour;
(2) enter into a forward contract to sell dollars and buy sterling in three months' time;
(3) purchase a 3-month sterling call option (the right to buy sterling and sell dollars).

Possible results:

1. If the exchange rate does move in the company's favour, then the company will receive a windfall profit on its long dollar position. However, this strategy is very dangerous because if the exchange rate moves contrary to the company's expectations, its sterling profits will be reduced and could become a loss as its costs are fixed in sterling.

2. If the company enters into a forward contract, it is locking in an exchange rate for the supply deal. This gives the company protection against a dollar depreciation but does not allow it to take any profit from a dollar appreciation, which is contrary to its expectations for the exchange rate.

3. If the company purchases a sterling call option, this will require the company to pay out a premium upfront. However, it will guarantee the company a minimum exchange rate for the supply contract. It allows the company to indulge its expectations that the dollar will appreciate from current levels as, should this expected appreciation occur, the company is free to abandon the option and transact in the market at the more favourable exchange rate.

If the company decides to purchase a currency option, it could buy a 3-month option, a European-style sterling call/dollar put option, with a strike price of £/$ 1.75 (that is, the right to buy sterling and sell dollars at a rate of £/$ 1.75). Assume the cost of the option is 1.74 % of the sterling amount, i.e. £ 99 428.57 ($ 10 000 000 divided by 1.75 equals £ 5 714 285.71 × 1.74 %).

The outcome at maturity is:

		Sterling amount from deal
Spot rate	*Option exercised/not exercised:*	*(less premium)*
1.8500	Exercised	£ 5 614 857.14
1.8000	Exercised	£ 5 614 857.14
1.7000	Not exercised – buy spot	£ 5 782 924.37
1.6500	Not exercised – buy spot	£ 5 961 177.49

14.7   HEDGING VERSUS SPECULATION

In viewing whether an option should be viewed as a hedge or as a speculative instrument, a hedger's main concern is the value of the option at maturity. For this reason, any fluctuation of the option's intrinsic value during its life is important, but any change in its time value is largely irrelevant.

> **Intrinsic value is the advantage to the holder of the option of the strike rate over the forward outright rate.**

Also, as the option is itself a hedge, no further hedging is required and therefore there are no extra costs.

The option premium for a hedger represents:

$$\text{Option premium} = \text{intrinsic value} + \text{time value}$$

For example, if the forward outright rate of the dollar against Swiss francs is 1.6000, then for a dollar call (right to buy), Swiss franc put (right to sell) option, with a strike of 1.5700, the intrinsic value of the option would be 0.0300 dollar against Swiss francs. For a dollar put (right to sell), Swiss franc call (right to buy) option, with a strike of 1.5700, then the intrinsic value of the option is 0.0000 dollar against Swiss francs.

Time value is a mathematical function of implied volatility, time to maturity, interest rate differentials, spot and the strike of an option.

Time value represents the additional value of an option due to the opportunity for the intrinsic value of the option to increase.

For a trader/speculator, the option premium represents the expected net present value of the cost of delta hedging the option.

A trader's main concern is the value of the option whenever it is marked to market. For this reason, any fluctuation in the intrinsic value of the option is important, but any change in the time value will also be significant. If the trader, at any time, decides to hedge or partially hedge the option, extra transaction costs may be incurred, which might affect the overall return.

14.8 OPTION THEORY

14.8.1 Delta

Delta is the change in premium per change in the underlying. Technically, the underlying is the forward outright rate, but as the option-pricing model assumes constant interest rates, this is often calculated using spot. For example, if an option has a delta of 25 and spot moved 100 basis points, then the option price gain/loss would be 25 basis points. For this reason, delta is sometimes thought of as representing the 'spot sensitive' amount of the option.

An option's price sensitivity to price changes in the underlying instrument is known as its delta.

Delta can also be thought of as the estimated probability of exercise of the option. As the option-pricing model assumes an outcome profile based around the forward outright rate, an **at-the-money** option has a delta of 50 %. It falls for **out-of-the-money** options and increases for **in-the-money** options, but the change is non-linear, in that it changes much faster when the option is close-to-the-money.

An option is said to be **delta-hedged** if a position has been taken in the underlying in proportion to its delta. For example, if one is short a call option on an underlying with a face value of $1 000 000 and a delta of 0.25, a long position of $250 000 in the underlying will leave one delta-neutral with no exposure to changes in the price of the underlying, but only if these are infinitesimally small.

The delta of an option is altered by changes in the price of the underlying and by its volatility, time to expiry, and interest rates. Hence, the delta hedge must be rebalanced frequently. This is known as delta-neutral hedging.

14.8.2   Gamma

> **Gamma is the rate of change in an option's delta for a one-unit change in the underlying.**

Gamma is the change in delta per change in the underlying and is important because the option model assumes that delta hedging is performed on a continuous basis. In practice, however, this is not possible as the market gaps and the net amounts requiring further hedging would be too small to make it worth while. The gapping effect that has to be dealt with in hedging an option gives the risk proportional to the gamma of the option.

An option's gamma is at its greatest when an option is at-the-money and decreases as the price of the underlying moves further away from the strike price. Therefore, gamma is U-shaped and is also greater for short-term options than for long-term options.

14.8.3   Volatility

> **It is a statistical function of the movement of an exchange rate. It measures the speed of movement within an exchange rate band, rather than the width of that band.**

In essence, volatility is a measure of the variability (but not the direction) of the price of the underlying instrument, essentially the chances of an option being exercised. It is defined as the annualized standard deviation of the natural log of the ratio of two successive prices.

Historical volatility is a measure of the standard deviation of the underlying instrument over a past period. **Implied volatility** is the volatility implied in the price of an option. All things being equal, higher volatility will lead to higher option prices. In traditional Black–Scholes models, volatility is assumed to be constant over the life of an option. Since traders mainly trade volatility, this is clearly unrealistic. New techniques have been developed to cope with volatility's variability. The best known are stochastic volatility, Arch and Garch. **Actual volatility** is the actual volatility that occurs during the life of an option. It is the difference between the actual volatility experienced during delta hedging and the implied volatility used to price an option at the outset, which determines if a trader makes or loses money on that option.

14.8.4   Time Decay (Theta)

Time decay is the effect of time passing on an option's value.

Theta is the depreciation of the time value element of the premium, that is, it measures the effect on an option's price of a one-day decrease in the time to expiration. The more the market and strike prices diverge, the less effect theta has on an option's price.

Obviously, if you are the holder of an option, this effect will diminish the value of the option over time, but if you are the seller (the writer) of the option, the effect will be in your favour, as the option will cost less to purchase. Theta is non-linear, meaning that its value decreases faster the closer the option is to maturity. Positive gamma is generally associated with negative theta, and vice versa.

14.8.5   American versus European

In circumstance where the option enables the purchase of a currency that yields a higher return than the currency that is given up in payment, these early exercise features have value, but in such cases, they are more expensive than their European-style counterparts. Examples where this is the case include currency options in which the call currency interest rate exceeds or is close to the put currency interest rate.

American-style option – an option a purchaser may exercise for early value at any time over the life of the option up to and including its expiration date.

European-style option – an option where the purchaser has the right to exercise only at expiration.

Hence, there is a price difference between the two styles of option, but only sometimes. The difference in price occurs because there is a difference in the interest rates that each currency attracts. With American options, the intrinsic value is priced against the spot or the forward outright price, whichever is the most advantageous. This is because the American option can be exercised for spot value at any time during its life. If the call currency (right to buy) of the option has a higher interest rate than the put currency (right to sell), there will be an advantage in calculating the intrinsic value against spot rather than against the forward outright rate. Therefore, the main risk of the writer of the American option is that at some point in time, if the option is so far in-the-money that there is negligible time value remaining, the holder may exercise early. This would mean that the writer would incur the differential interest cost of borrowing the higher interest rate currency and lending the lower interest rate currency. If this happens, the option is said to be at **logical exercise**.

As the American-style option is more flexible, shouldn't it always be more expensive? Actually, the American option is not really more flexible than the European option. True, it can be exercised early and therefore the intrinsic value can be realized immediately, but unless the option is at logical exercise, the holder would be better to sell the option back and receive the premium. (Remember, the premium represents the intrinsic value of an option plus time value.) This is true for both American and European options and, in both cases, if the option is not at logical exercise, and the aim is to realize maximum profit, it would be better to sell than to exercise the option.

Examples of cases when it would be better to pay extra premium and buy a more expensive American-style option are:

1. In buying an option where the call currency (right to buy) has the higher interest rate and it is expected that the interest rate differential will widen significantly.
2. In buying an option where the interest rates are close to each other and it is expected that the call (right to buy) interest rate will move above the put (right to sell) interest rate;
3. In buying an out-of-the-money option with interest rates as in (1) or (2), and it is expected that the option will move significantly into the money, then the American-style option is more highly leveraged and will produce higher profits.

14.9 PRICING THEORY

Theorists have devoted a substantial amount of work developing a mathematical model for pricing options and a number of different models exist as a result. All make certain assumptions about market behaviour, which are not totally accurate but which give the best solution to the price of an option. Although the formulae for pricing options is complex, they are all based on the same pricing principles.

The price of an option is made up of two separate components:

$$\text{Option premium} = \text{Intrinsic value} + \text{Time value}$$

There are six factors that contribute to this pricing of an option:

- prevailing spot price;
- interest rate differentials (forward rate);
- strike price;
- time to expiry;
- volatility;
- intrinsic value.

For European-style options, intrinsic value is the value of an option relative to the outright forward market price, i.e. it represents the difference between the strike price of the option and the forward rate at which one could transact today. Intrinsic value can be zero, but it is never negative.

The best-known original closed-form solution to option pricing was developed by Fischer Black and Myron Scholes in 1973 (Black–Scholes Model). In its simplest form, it offers a solution to pricing European-style options on assets with interim cash payouts over the life of the option. The model calculates the theoretical, or fair, value for the option by constructing an instantaneously riskless hedge – that is, one whose performance is the mirror image of the option payout. The portfolio of option and hedge can then be assumed to earn the risk-free rate of return.

Central to the model are the assumptions that (1) markets' returns are normally distributed (i.e. have log normal prices), (2) there are no transaction costs, (3) volatility and interest rates remain constant throughout the life of the option, and (4) the market follows a diffusion process. The model has the five major inputs: the risk-free interest rate, the options strike price, the price of the underlying, the option's maturity, and the volatility assumed. Since the first four are usually determined, markets tend to trade the implied volatility of the option.

For example, a 6-month European-style sterling put (right to sell), dollar call (right to buy) with the spot rate at $/£ 1.7500 and forward points of 515, giving an outright forward of 1.6985 (1.7500−0.0515), will have intrinsic value of 4.15 cents per pound.

If the strike price of the option is more favourable than the current forward price, the option is said to be **in-the-money**. If the strike price is equal to the forward rate, it is an **at-the-money** option, and if the strike price is less favourable than the outright forward, the option is termed **out-of-the-money**.

For American-style options, a similar definition applies, except that the option's 'moneyness' relative to the spot price also needs to be considered. Clearly, in the example above, an American-style option would be in-the-money relative to the forward but not to the spot. Conversely, if the option had the same details except that it was a call on sterling (right to buy), it would clearly be out-of-the-money under the European definition, but as an American-style option it would be in-the-money relative to the spot price. Naturally, the cost of the option would need to be considered in order to achieve a profitable early exercise.

14.10 OTHER CONSIDERATIONS

14.10.1 Market Conventions

How should one ask for an option price? The required pieces of information, in the preferred order, are as follows:

- The two currencies involved and which is the put and which is the call, e.g. dollar put, Swiss franc call.

- The period, e.g. two months or the expiry or delivery date, e.g. expiry 12 December, for delivery 14 December.
- The strike, e.g. 1.5010.
- The style, e.g. European or American style.
- The amount, e.g. 10 million dollars.

There are many ways of stating the period, but usually, if one date is stated, it is assumed to be the expiry date although it is always much safer to specify. In the same way, if a 10-day option is requested, it is assumes that the required option has an expiry date 10 days from the current date. If, however, an option is requested with a period in terms of months or years, e.g. three months, the dates of the option are worked out as follows:

- Calculate the spot date for that currency pair, using the same conventions as the spot market.
- Take the period, e.g. three months from that date, using the forward market conventions.

This gives the **delivery date**. The **expiry date** will then usually be two working days before that.

The exceptions occur in any currency pair where spot is not two working days, for example the Canadian dollar, where the expiry date would be one working day before the delivery date.

Note that with cross-currencies and dates involving American holidays, or in any case where there may be confusion, it is always best to quote both the expiry and delivery dates required.

In asking for an option price, always state the call currency and the put currency. For example, does a dollar/Swiss franc (USD/SFR) put mean a dollar put or a Swiss franc put? On the option exchanges and in the OTC interbank market, this would usually refer to a Swiss franc put/dollar call. However, most corporations would probably mean a dollar put. For this reason, always state the case in full, e.g. dollar call/Swiss franc put, or vice versa.

What does a live price mean? The price of an option is obviously dependent on the spot price in the market. As an option trader needs to delta hedge the option immediately, the spot at which the trader can hedge is the rate the trader uses to price the option. If a price is being quoted live it means that the person asking for the price will be quoted a premium price for the option, and the option trader will take the risk that spot moves during the transaction. The alternative to dealing live is to deal **with delta**. This means that the person asking the price will deal the delta hedge with the option trader as well as the option.

How is the premium normally quoted? Normally, the premium is quoted as a percentage of the base currency amount of the option. However, in the interbank market, it is normally quoted as pips per currency amount of the option. For example, if the option is a dollar/ Swiss franc option, the premium can be quoted in the following ways:

1. Percentage of the dollar amount of the option.
2. Percentage of the Swiss franc amount of the option.
3. Swiss franc pips per dollar amount of the option.
4. Dollar pips per Swiss franc amount of the option.

If the option were being dealt in a round amount of dollars, e.g. 10 million dollars, then either (1) or (3) would be the usual quote. If (2) or (4) were required, however, the Swiss franc amount of the option is found by multiplying the dollar amount by the strike of the option.

14.10.2 Premium Conversions

How can one form of premium be quoted to another? The following formula can be used, where BC is the base currency (commodity currency) and NBC is the non-base currency (terms currency):

1. % BC = % NBC × strike/spot
2. % NBC = % BC × spot/strike
3. NBC/BC = % NBC × strike
4. BC/NBC = % BC/strike.

For example, if a Swiss franc/dollar option costs 2.05 % dollar amount, spot is 1.5500 and the strike of the option is 1.5200, then

$$SFR/USD = 0.0205 \times 1.5500 = 0.031775$$

or

318 Swiss franc pips per dollar

14.10.3 Settlement

Normally, settlement takes place in full, e.g. if a dollar put (right to sell)/Swiss franc call (right to buy) option is exercised, the full amount of the dollars will be paid to the option writer and the exerciser will receive the full amount of Swiss francs from the option writer. As mentioned before, settlement takes place on the delivery date unless the option is American and has been exercised early, in which case settlement takes place spot from the date the option is exercised.

Is it necessary to settle both amounts in full? No – it is possible to 'net settle' the option. This means that only the profit on the option is paid from the writer to the

116   **A Foreign Exchange Primer**

holder of the option. If this is decided at the time of exercise, the writer will normally quote the holder a spot rate, and if this rate is acceptable, the option profit will be determined accordingly. If net settlement is agreed at the time of the original deal, it may be necessary to have a more formal arrangement for determining the profit on the option at the time of exercise.

How is an option exercised? It is sufficient that the option writer receives notice of exercise before the exercise time on the expiry date. This time is 1500 hours London time, 1500 hours Tokyo or 1000 hours New York time.

14.10.4   Risks

- **Credit risk** – In selling an option to a client, there is no real credit risk if the option expires worthless, i.e. it is not exercised. There is a transaction-related risk if it is exercised, which is similar to risk on a spot settlement thus requiring a credit line to be in place in advance of the transaction. The client pays an up-front premium.
- **Market price risk** – Because an option buyer enjoys the dual benefits of insurance and upside potential, the option writer is subject to a greater amount of market/price risk when it sells options than when it sells forward contracts. To compensate for this risk, the option writer charges the up-front premium.
- **Country risk** – Similar to that for forwards and swaps.

CONCLUDING REMARKS

In summary, options are not merely insurance contracts against exchange risk but they are above all financial assets that can be bought and sold just like tradable securities. Options may be combined so that their asymmetric payouts tailor a defined risk profile. Some combinations are primarily trading strategies, but option combinations can also be a useful tool – for example, for investors to construct a strategy allowing them to take advantage of a particular view that they have about a market direction. Other strategies allow purchasers to give up some of the benefits they may have received in market movements in return for a reduced premium payment. It must be remembered that buying a call and simultaneously selling a put with the same maturity date and the same strike is equivalent to entering into a forward contract. However, above all, remember the following risk profile of options:

Long option : unlimited profit potential − limited risk
Short option : unlimited risk − limited profit potential

15
Picturing Profit and Loss of Options

The illustration below (Figure 15.1) is used with each strategy. The diagram shows the profit/loss scale on the left vertical axis. The horizontal zero line in the middle is the break-even point. Therefore, anything above that line indicates a profit, anything below it, a loss. The scale along the bottom would represent the price of the underlying instrument, with lower prices to the left and higher prices to the right. A, B, C etc. in the diagrams indicates the strike price(s) involved.

15.1 LONG CALL

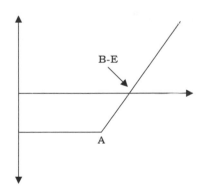

When to use
Very bullish on the market. The more bullish you are, the more out-of-the-money (higher) should be the option bought. No other position gives as much leveraged advantage in a rising market (with limited downside risk).

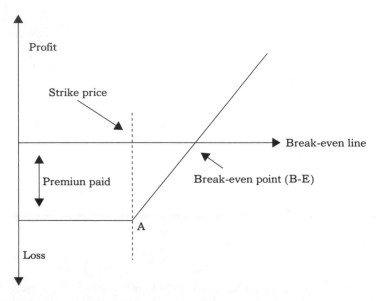

Figure 15.1 Profit and loss options

Profit characteristic
Profit increases as the market rises. At expiration, the break-even point will be the option strike price A plus the price paid for the option. For each point above the break-even point, the profit increases by an additional point.

Loss characteristic
The loss is limited to the amount paid for the option. Maximum loss is realized if the market ends below the strike price A. For each point above the strike price A, the loss decreases by an additional point.

Decay characteristic
The position is a wasting asset. As time passes, the value of the position erodes towards the expiration value. If volatility increases, erosion slows; as volatility decreases, erosion speeds up.

15.2   SHORT CALL

When to use
If you firmly believe that the market is not going up. Sell out-of-the-money (higher strike) options if you are only somewhat convinced; sell at-the-money options if you are very confident that the market will stagnate or fall. If you feel the market will fall sharply, sell in-the-money options for maximum profit.

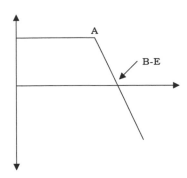

Profit characteristics
Profit is limited to the premium received. At expiration, the break-even point is strike price A plus premium received. Maximum profit is realized if the market settles at or below strike price A.

Loss characteristics
The loss increases as the market rises. At expiration, the losses increase by one point for each point the market is above the break-even point. Because the risk is open-ended, the position must be closely watched.

Decay characteristics
The position is a growing asset. As time passes, the value of the position increases as the option loses its time value. The maximum rate of increasing profits occurs if the option is at-the-money.

15.3   LONG PUT

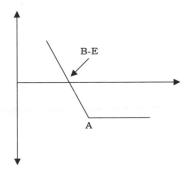

When to use
Very bearish on the market. The more bearish you are, the more out-of-the-money (lower) should be the option bought. No other position gives as much leveraged advantage in a falling market.

Profit characteristics
Profit increases as the market falls. At expiration, the break-even point will be the option strike price A minus the price paid for the option. For each point below the break-even point, the profit increases by an additional point.

Loss characteristics
The loss is limited to the amount paid for the option. Maximum loss is realized if the market ends above the option strike price A. For each point below the break-even point, the loss decreases by an additional point.

Decay characteristics
The position is a wasting asset. As time passes, the value of the position erodes towards the expiration value. If volatility increases, erosion slows; as volatility decreases, erosion speeds up.

15.4   SHORT PUT

When to use
If you firmly believe that the market is not going down. Sell out-of-the-money (lower strike) options if you are only somewhat convinced; sell at-the-money options if you are very confident that the market will stagnate or rise. If you think the market will only rise, sell in-the-money options for maximum profit.

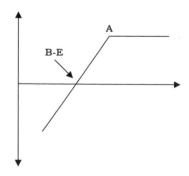

Profit characteristics
Profit is limited to the premium received. At expiration, the break-even point is strike price A minus premium received. Maximum profit is realized if the market settles at or above strike price A.

Loss characteristics
The loss increases as the market falls. At expiration, the losses increase by one point for each point the market is below the break-even point. Because the risk is open-ended, the position must be closely watched.

Decay characteristics
The position is a growing asset. As time passes, the value of the position increases as the option loses its time value. The maximum rate of increasing profits occurs if the option is at-the-money.

15.5   LONG STRADDLE

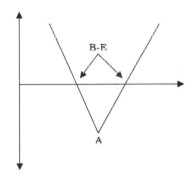

When to use
If the market is near A and it is expected to start moving but you are not sure which way. This is an especially good position if the market has been quiet, then starts to zigzag sharply, signalling a potential eruption. You should buy a call and a put at the same strike price A.

Profit characteristics
Profit is open-ended in either direction. At expiration, the break-even point is at strike price A plus or minus the cost of the combined premium. (However, the position is seldom held to expiration because of increasing decay levels with time.)

Loss characteristics
Loss is limited to the cost of the spread (the call–put spread). Maximum loss is incurred if the market is at A at expiration.

Decay characteristics
Decay accelerates as the options approach expiration. For this reason, the position is adjusted to neutrality by frequent profit taking. It is normally taken off well before expiration.

15.6   SHORT STRADDLE

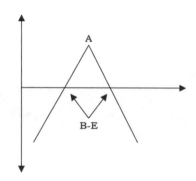

When to use
If the market is near strike price A and it is expected that the market is stagnating. Because you have short options, you reap the profits, in terms of premium retention, as they decay – as long as the market remains near strike price A. You would sell a call and a put at strike price A.

Profit characteristics
Profit is maximized if the market, at expiration, is at strike price A, i.e. premium received from. The break-even point is strike price A plus or minus that amount.

Loss characteristics
Loss potential is open-ended in either direction. The position, therefore, must be closely monitored and readjusted to neutrality if the market begins to drift away from strike price A. Only one option will be exercised, however.

Decay characteristics
Because you have short options, you pick up time-value decay at an increasing rate as expiration nears, maximized if the market is near strike price A.

15.7   LONG STRANGLE

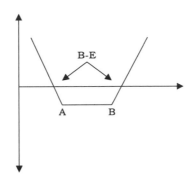

When to use
If the market is within or near an A–B range and has been stagnant. If the market explodes either way, money is made. If the market continues to stagnate, you lose less than with a long straddle. You should buy a put option with a strike price A and a call option with a strike price B.

Profit characteristics
Profit is open-ended in either direction. With the put A vs call B version (most common), break-evens are at strike price A minus the cost of the spread and strike price B plus the cost of the spread. Only one option will be exercised at expiration, however.

Loss characteristics
Loss is limited. In most common versions, loss is equal to the net cost of the position. Maximum loss is incurred if, at expiration, market is between strike prices A and B.

Decay characteristics
Decay accelerates as the options approach expiration, but not as rapidly as with a long straddle. To avoid the largest part of the decay, the position is normally taken off prior to expiration.

15.8   SHORT STRANGLE

When to use
If the market is within or near an A–B range and, though active, is quieting down. If the market goes into stagnation, you make money; if it continues to be active, you

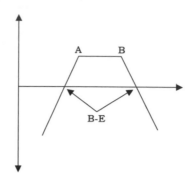

have a slightly smaller risk than with a short straddle. You should sell a put option at strike price A and a call option at strike price B.

Profit characteristics
Maximum profit equals the option receipts for the call and put. Maximum profit is realized if the market, at expiration, is between strike price A and strike price B.

Loss characteristics
At expiration, losses occur only if the market is above strike price B plus option receipts or below strike price A minus that amount. Potential loss is open-ended. The position is not riskless and only one side will be exercised.

Decay characteristics
Because you have only short options, you pick up time-value decay at an increasing rate as expiration nears, which is maximized if the market is within the A–B range.

15.9   BULL SPREAD

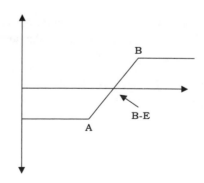

When to use
If you think the market will go up or, at least, is more likely to rise than to fall. This is a good position to have if you want to be in the market but are unsure of your bullish expectations. This is the most popular bullish trade. You should buy at strike price A and sell at strike price B.

Profit characteristics
Profit is limited, reaching a maximum if the market ends at or above strike price B at expiration. If a call-vs-call version (most common) is used, then the break-even point is at strike price A plus the net cost of the spread.

Loss characteristics
What is gained by limiting the profit potential is mainly a limit to loss if you made a wrong guess on the market. Maximum loss is if the market at expiration is at or below strike price A. With call-vs-call version, the maximum loss is the net cost of the spread.

Decay characteristics
If the market is midway between strike price A and strike price B, there is no time effect. At strike price B, profit is maximized. At strike price A, losses increase at maximum rate with time.

15.10   BEAR SPREAD

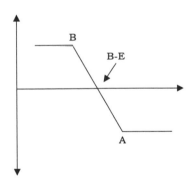

When to use
If you think the market will fall or, at least, is more likely to fall than to rise. It is the most popular position among bears because it may be entered as a conservative trade when you are uncertain about a bearish stance. You would buy at strike price A and sell at strike price B.

Profit characteristics

Profit is limited, reaching a maximum if the market ends at or below strike price B at expiration. If a put-vs-put version (most common) is used, then the break-even point is at strike price A minus the net cost of the spread.

Loss characteristics

By accepting a limit to profits, you gain a limit to risk. Losses at expiration increase as the market rises to strike price A, where they stabilize. With put-vs-put version, the maximum loss is the net cost of the spread.

Decay characteristics

If the market is midway between strike price A and strike price B, there is no time effect. At strike price B, profits are at a maximum. At strike price A, losses increase at a maximum rate with time.

15.11   LONG BUTTERFLY

When to use

One of the few positions which may be entered into advantageously in a long-term option series. You buy the 'wings' (strike prices A1 and A2) and sell the 'body' (straddle strike price B).

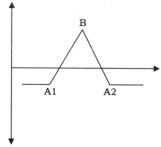

Note : B–A1 must equal A2–B

Profit characteristics

Maximum profit occurs if the market is at B at expiration. That profit would be B minus A minus cost of doing the spread. (This profit develops, almost totally, in the last month.)

Loss characteristics

Maximum loss, in either direction, is the cost of the spread. This is a very conservative trade, with break-even points at strike of call A1 plus the cost of the spread and at strike of put A2 minus the cost of the spread.

Decay characteristics
Decay is negligible until the final month, during which a distinctive pattern of butterfly forms. Maximum profit growth is at B, but if you are away from the A1–A2 range entering into the last month, then perhaps the option should be liquidated.

15.12   SHORT BUTTERFLY

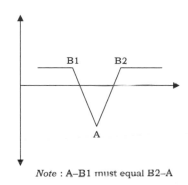

Note : A–B1 must equal B2–A

When to use
When the market is either below strike price B1 or above strike price B2 and the position is overpriced with approximately one month to run. Or, if, with only a few weeks left, the market is near A and it is expected that there will be an imminent move in either direction. You would buy the 'body' (straddle strike price A) and sell the 'wings' (strike call B1 and strike put B2).

Profit characteristics
Maximum profit is credit for which the spread is put on. This occurs when the market, at expiration, is below B1 or above B2, thus making all options in-the-money or all options out-of-the-money.

Loss characteristics
Maximum loss occurs if the market is at strike price A at expiration. Amount of that loss is A minus B1 minus credit received when setting up the position. Break-even points are at B1 plus initial credit and B2 minus initial credit.

Decay characteristics
Decay is negligible until the final month, during which the distinctive pattern of butterfly forms. Maximum loss acceleration is at A.

15.13   LONG CONDOR

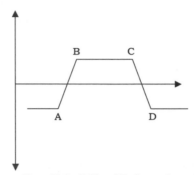

Note : B–A, C–B and D–C are all equal

When to use
Enter in far-out months, if desired. It is worth twice the average of A–B–C and B–C–D butterflies because it has twice the profit area.

Profit characteristics
Maximum profit is realized if the market is between strike price B and strike price C at expiration. For all-call or all-put versions, those profits equal B–A minus cost of options at set-up. Break-even points are at strike price A plus that cost and strike price D less that cost.

Loss characteristics
Maximum loss occurs if the market is below strike price A or above strike price D at expiration. For all-call or all-put versions, that loss is cost at set-up of the position.

Decay characteristics
Decay is negligible until the final month, during which the 'super butterfly' condor develops its characteristic shape. Maximum profits occur in the B–C range.

15.14   SHORT CONDOR

When to use
Normally entered into when the market, with less than one month to go, is between strike price B and strike price C, but you think there is good potential for a strong move outside of that range.

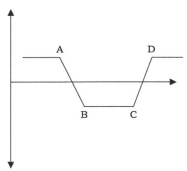

Note : B–A, C–B and D–C are all equal

Profit characteristics

Maximum profit will occur if the market is below strike price A or above strike price D at expiration. That profit, for all-put or all-call versions, will be credit received when the position is set-up.

Loss characteristics

Maximum loss will occur if the position is held to expiration and, at that time, the market is between strike price B and strike price C. For all-call or all-put versions, this amount to B–A – credit received.

Decay characteristics

Decay is negligible until the last month, during which a distinctive condor pattern emerges. Loss accelerates via decay with the market between B and C.

15.15   CALL RATIO SPREAD

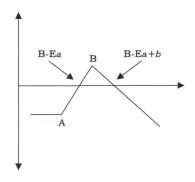

When to use
This spread is usually entered into when the market is near strike price A and the user expects a slight rise in the market but sees a potential for a sell-off. Buy strike price A and sell strike price B in twice the amount or some other ratio amount.

Profit characteristics
Maximum profit is at strike price B. Profit then decreases and only at break-even a + b is the position flat. Anything over break-even a + b represent a loss.

Loss characteristics
Loss is limited on the downside, but open-ended if the market rises. The rate of loss, if the market rises beyond B, is proportional to the number of excess shorts in the position, i.e. as determined by the initial ratio.

Decay characteristics
If the market is at strike price B, profits from option decay accelerates most rapidly with the passage of time. At strike price A, you have the greatest rate of loss accrual by the time decay of the long option.

15.16   PUT RATIO SPREAD

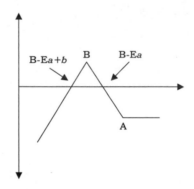

When to use
This strategy is usually entered into when the market is near strike price A and you expect the market to fall slightly but see a potential for a sharp rise. Buy a put strike price A and sell a put strike price B in twice the amount, or some other ratio amount.

Profit characteristics
Maximum profit is at strike price B. Profit then deteriorates so that at break-even a + b, the position is flat.

Loss characteristics
Loss limited on upside (to net cost of the position) but open-ended if the market falls. The rate of loss, if the market falls below B, is proportional to the number of excess shorts in the position.

Decay characteristics
If the market is at strike price B, profits from option decay accelerates most rapidly with the passage of time. At strike price A, you have the greatest rate of loss accrual the time by decay of the long option.

15.17 BARRIERS

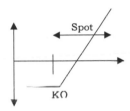

Out-of-the-money knock-out
A standard option that automatically cancels out if spot trades through a predetermined knock-out level. This level is set below the initial spot for a call option, and above spot for a put.

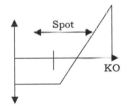

In-the-money knock-out
A standard option that automatically cancels out if spot trades through a predetermined knock-out level. This level is set above the initial spot for a call option, and below spot for a put.

Double Knock-Out
A standard option that automatically cancels out if spot trades through either one of two predetermined knock-out levels. One of the knock-out levels is set above the initial spot and the other one below spot – hence there is both an out-of-the-money and an in-the-money knock-out with these options.

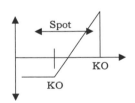

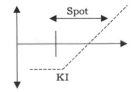

Out-of-the-money knock-in
A standard option that can only be exercised upon expiry providing that spot has previously traded through a predetermined knock-in level. This level is set below the initial spot for a call option and above spot for a put.

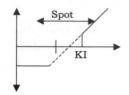

In-the-money knock-in

A standard option that can only be exercised upon expiry providing that spot has previously traded through a predetermined knock-in level. This level is set above the initial spot for a call option and below spot for a put.

Knock-in/knock-out

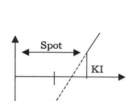

A standard option that automatically cancels out if spot trades through a predetermined knock-out level and, in addition, can only be exercised upon expiry providing that spot has previously traded through a predetermined knock-in level. The knock-out level is set below the initial spot for a call option and above spot for a put. Similarly, the knock-in level is set above spot for a call and below spot for a put.

Glossary of Terms for Chapters 14 and 15

American option   An option which may be exercised at any time.

Assignment   Notification to the option writer requiring that person to fulfil his or her contractual obligations to buy or sell the currency.

At-the-money forward   An option with an exercise price equal to the currency forward rate.

At-the-money spot   An option with an exercise price equal to the currency spot rate.

Bear spread   An option strategy designed to allow the trader to participate, with limited profit and limited risk, in the decline of a currency.

Break-even point   The foreign exchange rate or currency futures price at which a strategy neither makes nor loses money.

Bull spread   An option strategy designed to allow the trader to participate, with limited risk and limited return, in the rise of a currency.

Butterfly spread   A combination of a bull spread and a bear spread; the strategy normally gives a maximum return and maximum loss.

Calendar spread   A strategy involving the buying and selling of options with different expiration dates.

Call option   An option which gives the holder the right to buy, and the writer the obligation to sell, a predetermined amount of a currency to a predetermined date at a predetermined exchange rate.

Clearing corporation   An organization which matches and guarantees option trades on an exchange.

Combination   A strategy involving the buying of call and put options with different strikes but with the same expiration dates.

Condor spread   A variation on a butterfly spread but with strikes further apart.

Conversion arbitrage   A riskless strategy involving the buying of a currency and the simultaneous buying of a put and writing of a call option, both normally European style and of the same strikes and expiration.

Covered write   A strategy involving the buying of a currency and the writing of a call option, or the selling of a currency and the writing of a put option.

Credit premium   The premium received when an option is written.

Debit premium   The premium paid when an option is purchased.

Delta   The ratio by which the price of the option moves relative to the underlying spot or futures contract.

Delta spread (trade or hedge)   A trade involving the adjustment of the long or short options positions by the ratio of the delta.

Discount   Term used to describe an option trading for less than its intrinsic value.

Downside protection   For covered calls, the 'cushion' against loss provided by the option premium received.

Early exercise   The exercise of an option before its expiration date.

European option   An option which may only be exercised on the expiration day.

Exchange-traded market   The organized marketplace for option trading purposes.

Exercise   Process by which the holder of an option elects to take delivery of (call) or deliver (put) a currency according to the contract terms.

Exercise price   The price at which the option holder has the right to buy or sell the underlying currency or currency futures contract.

Expiration cycle   In the exchange-traded options market, the time frame in which listed options run.

Expiration date   The last day on which a holder can exercise his or her option.

Expiration time   In the over-the-counter market the latest time an option may be exercised is usually 3 p.m. London time, 10 a.m. New York time, or 3 p.m. Tokyo time, on that particular day.

Fair value   Usually refers to the value of an option premium according to a mathematical model.

Gamma   The change in the delta for a unit change in the spot price.

Hedge ratio   The ratio of options to buy or sell against a spot position in order to create a riskless hedge.

Implied volatility   The expected standard deviation of percentage price changes.

In-the-money   An option that has intrinsic value. For a call, the strike is below the spot rate. For a put, the strike is above the spot rate.

Intrinsic value   The value of an option, were it to be exercised immediately.

Leg   One component of a multiple option strategy.

Margin   Initial margin is the amount required to be put up as collateral by the option writer to the clearing corporation. It is equivalent to a performance bond. Variation or maintenance margin is further cover required, should the option position move against the writer.

Mark to market   Daily adjustment of an account to reflect accrued profits and losses.

Money spread   Strategy involving the buying and writing of options with different strikes but with the same expiration dates. It can be put on for a credit or debit to take advantage of a directional market move.

Naked position   A short option position which is not covered by the underlying currency or with another option.

Out-of-the-money   An option with no intrinsic value. For a call, the strike is above the spot rate and for a put the strike is below the spot rate.

Over-the-counter market   Customized option market usually traded directly between banks and their customers or with other banks.

Premium   The amount of money paid by a buyer and received by a seller for an option.

Put option   An option giving the holder the right to sell and the writer the obligation to buy, a predetermined amount of currency to a predetermined date at a predetermined exchange rate.

Ratio spread   Strategy involving the sale of an amount of call options in excess of the amount of a long call option position held, or the sale of put options in excess of the amount of a long put option position held.

Ratio write   Strategy involving the sale of call options in excess of the amount of a long currency position held, or the sale of put options in excess of the amount of a short currency position held.

Reversal arbitrage   Riskless trade involving the selling of a currency and the simultaneous buying of a currency call and writing of a currency put option, both normally European style and of the same strikes and expiration.

Settlement date   Two business days following exercise. It is the day on which the currencies involved in the option transaction are exchanged.

Spread   Strategy involving the simultaneous buying and selling of options on the same currency.

Straddle   Strategy involving the buying of call and put options with the same strikes and maturity.

Strangle   Strategy involving the buying of call and put options with different strikes but with the same expiration dates.

Strike   The price at which the option holder has the right to buy or sell the underlying currency or currency futures contract.

Theta   The change in the premium for a unit change in time.

Time value   The amount by which an option premium exceeds its intrinsic or in-the-money value.

Vega   The change in the premium for a unit change in implied volatility.

Volatility   The standard deviation of percentage price changes.

Writer   One who sells an option.

16
Foreign Exchange Futures

Although futures contracts on commodities have been traded on organized exchanges since the 1860s, financial futures are relatively new, dating from the introduction of foreign currency futures in 1972, not long after President Nixon closed the gold window and before many currencies had achieved free-floating status. Then, foreign exchange futures traded on a floor with trading limited to regular trading hours during the day. Now, however, most trading has moved to the Chicago Mercantile Exchange (CME) Globex electronic trading platform where volumes have been booming over the past few years.

The basic form of the futures contract is identical to that of the forward contract, whereby a futures contract obligates its owner to purchase a specified asset at a specified exercise price on the contract maturity date. Likewise, currency futures are defined as a standardized contract/agreement to sell or buy a specific amount of a currency at a particular price on a stipulated future date.

> A future is a contract to buy and sell a standard quantity of a given instrument, at an agreed price, on a given date.

As mentioned in previous chapters, cash foreign exchange trading offers numerous advantages, such as low cost entry, high leverage, real-time quotes to trade and no commissions or fees. With foreign exchange futures trading, there are some other advantages to take note of. Firstly, there is one central market, where the bids and offers are channeled into one place, establishing one price that is widely distributed the instant a trade occurs. Secondly, there are tight bid/offer spreads. With everyone coming into one market place at any one time, the foreign exchange futures provide sizeable liquidity and a smooth flow of trading from one price to another, resulting in the bid/ask spread being narrowed. Thirdly, there is transparent pricing, meaning that the current price arrived at by these multiple sources is available to all traders of all sizes at the same time. Today, with electronic trading, there is no discrimination – the small trader is on an equal footing with large traders on a level playing field. In addition, all prices and costs associated with trading foreign exchange futures are openly disclosed. Finally, there is no counter-party risk, as the exchange's clearing organization is actually the counter-party to every trade, setting the rules and policies to preserve the honesty of the market and to provide a verified record of all trading activity that can be audited, if necessary.

Today, pit trading is fading fast with an estimated 50 % of all futures markets transactions in 2007 occurring via automated trading strategies, including market-making and quantitative black-box trading activities. According to some recent surveys, this proportion could well rise to 90 % by 2010, mostly due to IT-literate traders entering the futures market with sophisticated trading technology being adopted. In fact, it has been reported that overall in 2007, over 144 million FX contracts with a notional value of over $ 17.9 trillion was traded at the CME. The CME's Euro foreign exchange futures continued to be the most actively traded foreign exchange contract with an average daily volume of 170 210 contracts; this represents a notional value of $ 29.2 billion, which was up 6 % over 2006. Futures on the New Zealand dollar, Australian dollar, and Japanese yen experienced the strongest growth rates with daily volumes up 75 %, 64 % and 57 % respectively when compared with 2006.

16.1   TWO-SIDED RISK

Like a forward contract, the futures contract has a two-sided risk. However, in marked contrast to forwards, credit or default risk can be virtually eliminated in a futures market. Firstly, instead of conveying the value of a contract through a single payment at maturity, any change in the value of a futures contract is conveyed at the end of the day in which it is realized. For example, suppose that, on the day after origination, the financial price rises and, consequently, the financial instrument has a positive value. In the case of a forward foreign exchange contract, this value change would not be received until maturity. With a futures contract, this change in value is received at the end of the day. In the language of the futures markets, the futures contract is **cash-settled** or **marked-to-market** daily.

Since the value of the futures contract is paid or received at the end of each day, a futures contract can be likened to a series of forward contracts. That is, a futures contract is like a sequence of forwards in which the 'forward' contract written on day 0 is settled on day 1 and is replaced, in effect, with a new 'forward' contract reflecting the new day 1 expectations. This new contract is itself settled on day 2 and replaced, and so on until the day the contract ends.

In other words, a futures contract can be thought of as 'rolling over' forward contracts on a daily basis. Strictly speaking, the futures price and the forward price are not quite the same but as a practical matter they are so close that little accuracy is lost in viewing them as identical. Therefore, analogous to forward contracts, the futures price is that contract price which results in the futures contract having zero value to both the buyer and the seller each day the contract is settled and restruck.

Secondly, all market participants, sellers and buyers alike, post a performance bond, i.e. margin. If a futures contract increases in value during the trading day, this gain is added to the margin account at the end of the day. Conversely, if the contract loses value, this loss is deducted from the margin account. If the margin account balance falls below some agreed-upon minimum, the holder will be required to post an additional bond. Hence, the margin account must be replenished or the holder's position will be closed out.

16.2   EXCHANGE MEMBERS

There are two types of exchange members who can trade any futures contract. First, there are commission brokers, or floor brokers, who execute orders for non-members. These orders from non-members will originate through futures commission merchants – which are usually organizations, for example, brokers and commercial banks. These types of organizations will solicit orders for futures trading. Futures commission merchants also hold their clients' margin monies and handle all margin accounting. The floor broker executing the order may or may not be affiliated with the futures commission merchant that originated the order.

The second type of exchange member is called a 'local', and is simply an individual trading for his or her own account. Essentially, locals are willing to hold positions, inter- or intra-day, acting much like a market maker who hopes to profit from the bid–offer spread or market moves.

16.3   CLEARING CORPORATION

An important feature of an organized futures exchange is the Clearing Corporation. Essentially, the Clearing Corporation interposes itself as the seller to every buyer and the buyer to every seller. In other words, the Clearing Corporation becomes the counterparty to every trade, guaranteeing the opposite side of every transaction. This has several attractive features:

- Firstly, the buyer of a futures contract need not be concerned with the creditworthiness of the seller. If the buyer's position is doing well, i.e. the futures price is rising, then the buyer is guaranteed the daily receipt of the variation margin by the Clearing Corporation, independent of whether the original seller was able to pay that same variation margin. In this example, the Clearing Corporation looks to the member firm, who originated the futures sale, for the timely payment of the daily variation margin independent of whether the original seller has paid sufficient margin into the account.

- Secondly, the margin accounting problem is significantly simplified. There is now only one entity with which the member firm must deal in settling margin calls, as opposed to having to exchange monies with all other member firms.
- In addition, the Clearing Corporation will net out all margin calls and receipts for a single member firm across all of that firm's positions, such that only one net amount of funds must be transferred at the end of each trading day.

16.3.1 Major Exchanges

The major exchanges for financial futures include the Chicago Board of Trade (CBT), the Chicago Mercantile Exchange (CME), the International Monetary Market (IMM), the London International Financial Futures Exchange (LIFFE), the New York Futures Exchange (NYFE) and the Kansas City Board of Trade (KC).

16.4 QUOTING CURRENCY FUTURES

How are currency futures quoted? Generally, in the foreign exchange market, currencies are quoted against the American dollar. For example, a rate of 1.67 Swiss francs per dollar means that it takes 1.67 Swiss francs to buy/sell one dollar. Of course, there are the exceptions to this rule, for example sterling. However, currency futures are priced in American terms, in that it quotes how many dollars it takes to buy one unit of foreign currency. They are the reciprocal of those used in the cash market. Thus a rate of 1.67 Swiss francs per dollar would be quoted in the futures market as 0.5988 dollars per Swiss franc (1 divided by 1.67), which means that it costs 60 cents to buy one Swiss franc. For each contract, there is a specific contract size, for example one Swiss franc contract is worth 125 000 francs, the Japanese yen is worth 12 500 000 yen, sterling is worth 62 500 pounds, while the euro is worth 125 000 euros.

16.5 TICKS AND DELIVERY MONTHS

The minimum price movement of a currency futures contract is called a **tick**. The value of a tick is determined by multiplying the minimum tick size by the size of the contract. For example, using the Swiss franc against the dollar, 1-point is $ .0001 per Swiss franc, which equals $ 12.50 per contract, while 1-point sterling is worth $ .0001 per pound, which equals $ 6.25 per contract. The contract trading months are on the same quarterly cycle as other financial instruments: March, June, September and December. They are also known as the delivery months, because the seller of a contract must be prepared to deliver the specified amount of foreign currency to the buyer if the seller has not cancelled the obligation with an offsetting purchase. It must be said that the vast majority of market participants close out their positions before delivery.

16.6   CONTRACT SPECIFICATIONS

Today, there are 41 individual foreign exchange futures and 31 options products, covering major currency pairs as well as an array of emerging market currencies, but some examples of contract specifications for currencies against the dollar futures are listed below.

Product	*Trading unit and point description*
Australian dollar	100 000 dollars – physically delivered 1 point = $ 0.0001 per dollar = $ 10.00 per contract
Brazilian real	100 000 real – cash settled $1/2$ point = $ 0.0005 per real = $ 5.00 per contract
British pounds	62 500 pounds – physically delivered 1 point = $ 0.0001 per pound = $ 6.25 per contract
Canadian dollars	100 000 dollars – physically delivered 1 point = $ 0.0001 per dollar – $ 10.00 per contract
Euro	125 000 euros – physically delivered 1 point = $ 0.0001 per euro = $ 12.50 per contract
Japanese yen	12 500 000 yen – physically delivered 1 point = $ 0.000001 per yen = $ 12.50 per contract
Mexican peso	500 000 peso – physically delivered 1 point = $ 0.00001 per peso = $ 5.00 per contract
New Zealand dollars	100 000 dollars – physically delivered 1 point = $ 0.0001 per dollar = $ 10.00 per contract
'New' Russian ruble	2 500 000 ruble – cash settled 1 point = $ 0.00001 per ruble = $ 25.00 per contract
South African rand	500 000 rand – physically settled 1 point = $ 0.00001 per rand = $ 5.00 per contract
Swiss franc	125 000 franc – physically delivered 1 point = $ 0.0001 per franc = $ 12.50 per contract
Swedish krona	2 000 000 krona – physically delivered 1 point = 0.00001 dollar/krona = $ 20.00 per contract
Norwegian krone	2 000 000 krone – physically delivered 1 point = 0.00001 dollar/krone = $ 20.00 per contract

16.7   EUROPEAN STYLE OPTIONS

Currently, the CME offers European style options on a limited number of currencies (euro, Japanese yen, British pound, Canadian dollar and Swiss franc futures contracts) whereby these options, if in-the-money, are automatically exercised at expiration. European style options are used by most options traders in the OTC FX markets. Because there is no risk of early exercise, they are often priced lower than American style options.

Just like foreign exchange futures contracts, these European style options have set contract terms. For example, minimum tick size, regular strikes, initial strikes listed, price limits, expiration months, expiration day, termination of trading, delivery, exercise and trading hours.

Options on futures are among the most versatile risk management products offered by the CME. They can be used to limit downside risk and maximize upside profits. As a result, they have become an increasingly popular hedging vehicle, and are used today by corporations, bankers, professional and retail foreign exchange traders and equity portfolio managers. Additionally, this market offers easy access and liquid markets, where treading is via open outcry on the trading floor and electronically via CME Globex virtually around the clock throughout the trading week.

Looking at recent reports, foreign exchange contract volumes jumped by 26 % at The CME in 2007, to 569 671 contracts a day. This increase was led by foreign exchange options on futures, which grew by 31 % to 17 100 contracts per day reflecting a notional value of $ 2.4 billion a day. In addition, electronic trading of options over CME Globex increased more than fivefold, with an average electronic daily volume of 7769 contracts.

Besides being able to trade foreign exchange futures options on The CME, the International Securities Exchange (ISE), which is the largest equity options exchange in the world, launched foreign exchange options trading in the second quarter of 2007. The ISE operates a family of fully electronic trading platforms and is a wholly owned subsidiary of Eurex, a leading global derivatives exchange. ISE FX Options are exchange-listed securities that have US dollar based underlying value similar to traditional equity or index options. However, at the moment, there are only four currency pairs: British pound, Canadian dollar, European euro and Japanese yen.

CONCLUDING REMARKS

In summary, a foreign exchange futures contract is a forward contract for standardized currency amounts and for standard value dates. Buyers and sellers of foreign exchange futures are required to post initial margin or security deposits for each contract. Participants also have to pay brokerage commissions that can be fixed or negotiated depending on the size of the trade. Foreign exchange futures are only traded on regulated exchanges. In general, futures are used by banks, commodity trading advisers and arbitrage houses, i.e. by 'professional' traders rather than by corporations.

It should be remembered that the major difference between the foreign exchange futures and the foreign exchange 'cash' market is that the futures market settles gains and losses on a daily basis through the margin mechanism where an actual cash flow ensues. In the cash market, a cash flow only arises at the maturity of a transaction. Even though most participants will revalue their foreign exchange cash forward position on a daily basis, i.e. mark-to-market, all gains and losses occur on paper only, until a trade is finally settled.

Choosing between foreign exchange futures contracts and forward foreign exchange contracts for managing currency exchange rate risk involves consideration of a number of trade-offs. As noted in previous chapters, forwards lock in a prospective exchange rate with virtual certainty. On the other hand, foreign exchange futures contracts will foster approximately that same exchange rate. The source of risk for the futures contract pertains to the uncertainty associated with the size of the basis at the time the futures hedge needs to be liquidated. Depending on prevailing interest rate differentials in the market at that time, this uncertainty may prove to be beneficial or adverse.

In addition, foreign exchange futures provide greater flexibility in that they are more easily offset than forwards if the need for hedging is no longer required. Furthermore, foreign exchange futures have the ancillary benefit that they do not introduce any added credit risk for the hedger as a consequence of the rigorously practiced marking-to-market requirement, while foreign exchange forwards do.

17
Exchange for Physical

An exchange for physical (EFP) refers to exchanging a physical (cash) position for a futures position. This is where a spot interbank transaction can be converted into a futures position via an exchange for physical. Consequently, when a cash position is exchanged for a future position, the EFP is simply a mechanism by which the cash position is converted to its IMM or Finex equivalent. The EFP represents the current spot (cash) price plus or minus the interest rate differential (cost of carry) between the two currencies, expressed in the futures price, and it is essentially an **ex-pit** transaction.

17.1 EXAMPLES

17.1.1 Example 1

In this example, the mechanics of an EFP transaction would be where on, say, 13 December the interbank spot price for francs for value 15 December is 1.6700 bid–offer 1.6705. The market user sells 25 million Swiss francs at 1.6705 for value 15 December and then decides to convert the short cash position of 25 million Swiss francs to the IMM equivalent for short contracts for March. Assume the forward pips for 3-month $/Sfr is 1.7/1.9. The resulting transaction can be viewed as:

> buys Sfr 25 million at 1.6705 value 15 December
> sells 200 March IMM contracts at 0.5986
> (1.6705 + 1.9 = 1.67069 and then 1 divided by 1.67069, giving 0.5986)

The result for the cash position is:

> short Sfr 25 million at 1.6705 value 15 December
> long Sfr 25 million at 1.6705 value 15 December

so that the net cash position is flat and the market user is left with an open IMM futures position of being short 200 March IMM futures contracts at 0.5986.

17.1.2   Example 2

1. On 13 December, the interbank spot price for British pounds for value 15 December was 1.5000 bid–offer 1.5005.
2. The trader sells £ 10 million (equivalent of 160 IMM contracts) at 1.5000 value 15 December.
3. The trader decides to convert the short cash position of £ 10 million to the IMM equivalent of short 160 contracts for March.

In the resulting transaction the dealer interbank swap price for 16 March is 70–67, thus the trader executes a simultaneous swap transaction:

> buys £ 10 million at 1.5000 value 15 December and
> sells 160 March IMM contracts at 1.4930 (1.5000 − 0.0070)

Hence, the result is:

> short £ 10 million at 1.5000 value 15 December and
> long £ 10 million at 1.5000 value 15 December.

This results in a net cash position which is flat (square) and the trader is short 160 March IMM futures contracts at 1.4930.

17.2   POINT OF THE EXERCISE

The whole point of the exercise is that the client's spot cash position is flat and no profit or loss will be generated. The client, however, will have a futures position at only one average price for the full amount traded. The EFP transaction is 'posted' on the required exchange. Also, there are no commissions or fees charged on the cash side of the transaction, as shown in Table 17.1.

CONCLUDING REMARKS

Briefly, the EFP process is generally used by market participants who want to execute a trade 'over the counter' (OTC) and want to convert it into a foreign exchange futures contract (or vice versa). They can be traded as opening or as closing trades. To offset a foreign exchange futures position or to be treated as an open foreign exchange

Table 17.1   Interbank versus futures

Interbank spot	IMM futures
Single counterparty risk	Counterparty risk with Exchange
Unregulated market	Regulated market
Tailored maturity dates	Limited delivery months
Tailored currency amounts	Specific contract specifications
Greater liquidity	Lower average volume
Single average price	Multiple price fills
No exchange fees	
No reporting levels	
Unrealized gains can only be withdrawn upon maturity date	

futures position, a cash trade has to be converted into a foreign exchange futures contract and the deal must be posted on the exchange. An EFP is nothing more than the transfer of a contract to the futures exchange clearing house.

With the EFP execution, the main points are that the client's spot cash position is flat. No profit or loss will be generated. The client will have a futures position at only one average price for the full amount traded. With the execution of the EFP, the futures price will be posted (reported) to the exchange and the client will receive a confirmation, as he or she would for an IMM or Finex transaction. Additionally, fees and commissions will be recorded in exactly the same manner as if the transaction was executed on any of the exchanges.

Part III
Essential Knowledge

18
Foreign Exchange Dealing Rooms

Ever since the market experienced problems of unauthorized dealing, fraud and collusion in several institutions in the early 1970s, banks and institutions have been encouraged by their regulatory authorities to impose strict rules and regulations on the type of business transacted, its controls and the manner in which it is monitored. One of the most important aspects in the control of a dealing operation is the division of duties between dealing and back-office processing. Dealers should (a) effect the deals in the interbank market, or with clients, (b) maintain sufficient informal records as required to monitor their positions, (c) complete a source document (deal ticket) and, from that moment on, have no further part in or control over the processing, confirmation or settlement procedures involved.

18.1 COMPOSITION OF A DEALING ROOM

The composition of an institution's dealing room very much depends on that institution's size, its spread of market interests and its client base (see Figure 18.1). However, in general, the majority of institutions actively involved in the foreign exchange markets will have some or all of the personnel listed below.

18.1.1 Spot Dealers

Spot dealers are the dealing section the media love the most. Whenever there is pressure on any currency, that pressure will be most noticeable on the currency's spot value. They are market makers.

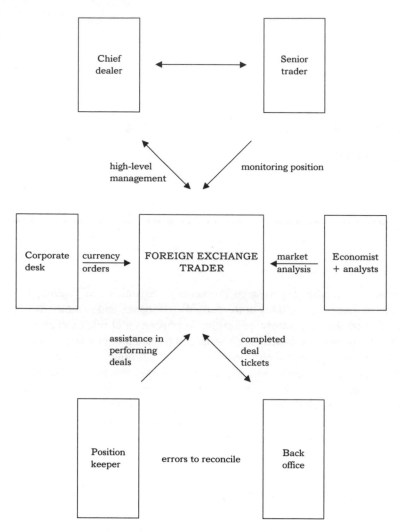

Figure 18.1 Graphic example of the relationship between all the different personnel in a dealing room

18.1.2 Forward Dealers

Forward dealers will normally be active market makers in the same major currencies as traded by the spot dealers. Here, rather than dealing on the minute-by-minute value of the currency, forward dealers are looking at the relative currency interest rates over the standard forward period dates quoted by the market.

18.1.3   Money-market Dealers

Money-market dealers control the interbank deposit and loan positions of the bank. The interbank market deals in all periods from overnight (depending on currency) to one-year funds and above. They are also responsible for funding the bank's commercial asset portfolio.

18.1.4   Treasury Product Dealers

Treasury product dealers are involved in numerous other activities, involving other financial instruments and newer off-balance-sheet products. Some of the treasury products lend themselves to trading activities (futures, options, etc.), while others are offered by the treasury products dealers as a customer service in-house, to providing assistance wherever it is needed in the management of all types of financial risk.

18.1.5   Corporate Dealers

Corporate dealers undertake a totally different role to that of the interbank dealers. In most situations, they will not make a market, but will instead obtain rates from the market makers in response to their client's dealing requests and quote for those accordingly. They are, in effect, the 'middle men' between the market makers and the clients. In their own right, they have a tremendous marketing role to play as in many respects they are the front-line representatives of the institution.

18.1.6   Research Personnel

Research personnel, generally, have a presence on the trading floor because they assist the traders in their task with technical and statistical research, market commentaries and graphical analyses, among other things.

18.1.7   Position Clerks

Position clerks are the workhorses of the dealing room, as they tend to carry out all of the clerical functions that require immediate execution.

18.2   BACK OFFICE

In most institutional organizations, the term 'back office' is generally accepted as a
description of all processing functions connected with a dealing operation outside
the actual dealing itself. The back office starts, therefore, at the dealing room door
and is a vital part of any dealing room function. It is concerned with settlement
of trades, confirmations, maturity files and reconciliations. Other departments are
financial control and information technology.

19
Managing the Relationship with an Institution

In today's volatile markets, it is becoming increasingly important that salespeople, corporate foreign exchange dealers, corporate foreign exchange advisers or international treasury advisers (various titles depending on the organization) keep themselves abreast of developments in the markets. More often than not, corporate treasurers, in particular, but also speculators, will use a small number of people who are constantly in touch with them, to advise accordingly on market developments. For such a relationship to work smoothly, it is advisable that both parties establish at the onset some ground rules – namely, what each party expects from the another. In general, the following should be expected from an adviser:

- regular market updates;
- prompt and timely response to enquiries, questions and issues relating to treasury risk management;
- sound advice on hedging strategies based on fundamental and technical analysis.

In return, the adviser needs the following to enhance the quality of service:

- knowledge of the individual's philosophy to risk management;
- the client's exposure situation – inflows/outflows by currency and timing;
- short-term or long-term trading strategy;
- legal/tax constraints, if any.

19.1 ROLE OF THE ADVISER

Once the prerequisites of the relationship have been established, the adviser will have to demonstrate an overall understanding of the foreign exchange market to earn the trust of the client. However, clients must recognize that they and only they are responsible for any trading decision. The adviser is only an adviser, for good or bad.

One role of the adviser that is often under-utilized is that of market watcher. By physically being located in the institution's dealing room, the adviser can follow the market very closely. The client, on the other hand, on many occasions, has to leave and will not be able to watch the markets. Thus, one of the adviser's functions is to 'watch' a price level. In fact, the client can even leave an order with the adviser for execution once the necessary conditions are met. As a client, you can be assured that the adviser will work for your interest. You are the client and the adviser wants to get your business, but as the institution pays the adviser, he or she needs to make money for the institution. You can assist advisers by dealing with them if their prices are market prices, and, even at times, by dealing when their prices are slightly off. There is a premium for quality service. The better the service, the more the client benefits.

19.2 CLIENT–ADVISER RELATIONSHIP

As the salesperson or adviser or corporate trader, etc., will be the primary contact between a market maker and the client, this relationship is illustrated in Figure 19.1.

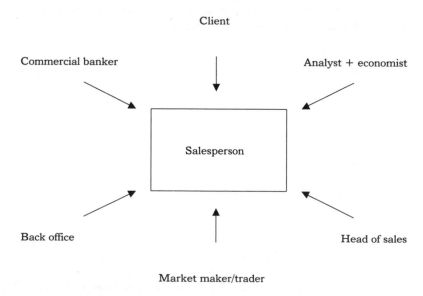

Figure 19.1 Client–adviser relationship

19.3   MARKETING PROCESS

Institutions with established client relationships will continue to expand their client lists by carefully selecting suitable targets. The marketing process for financial services is summarized graphically in Figure 19.2.

Figure 19.2   The marketing process

20
Foreign Exchange Dealings

Today, dealings in the foreign exchange market are usually done over the telephone or via the Internet. The Internet is a very quick and easy way to make a foreign exchange transaction, with 'click and deal' or 'request for price' systems dominating. However, the majority of all trading is still transacted over the telephone. Use of the telephone allows for prompt and timely execution, but also leaves room for errors in communication.

20.1 ASKING FOR A QUOTE

When asking for a quote, the following basic information needs to be conveyed to the market maker directly or to a corporate foreign exchange dealer: type of transaction, currency pair, and quantity. For example, a client would say:

'I want to buy Sfr 5 million value spot – what is your quote please?'

Today, a market maker normally quotes a **two-way** price, where the trader stands ready to bid for, or offer up to, some standard amount. The difference between the two prices is the **spread**. Market convention, where trading is between market 'professionals', is not to quote the **big figures**. Instead, a trader tends to quote only the last two figures of the price, the **pips**. For example, if the rate of dollars against the yen were 123.35/40, then the trader would only quote 35/40. That is, the trader bids for dollars at 123.35 and offers dollars at 123.40. If a client is checking prices with other market makers, then the client should inform the trader by saying that it is at his **risk**, i.e. the quote can be changed by the trader. The client should then ask when a new price is needed. If the client wishes to deal, then the trader's price would be **hit**, that is, where one side of the price or the other is accepted. Written confirmation of this deal, whether oral or electronic, will be exchanged and instructions taken as to whether this trade is to be settled or not and the currency amounts are transferred into the designated accounts on the value date.

20.2   EXAMPLES

20.2.1   Example 1

XYZ Corporation, based in Japan, needs to raise dollars to pay for a delivery of machine parts from America. The treasurer gets in contact with his bank dealer to arrange to buy the dollars in the spot market. The treasurer's screens display indicative prices contributed by certain major banks. This gives the treasurer a good idea of the current exchange rate. However, this is only an **indicative rate** and it is not a dealable price, i.e. not a price on which to deal. Therefore, the following steps are taken:

Treasurer: Please quote me dollar/yen in 10 million dollars. (At this stage there is no mention of whether the client wants to buy or sell dollars.)
Dealer: 52/57.
Treasurer: I buy 10 million dollars.
Dealer: To confirm, you buy 10 million dollars against yen at 123.57 value spot.

At this stage, the dealer fills in a deal ticket with the details of the trade including currencies, amount, which currency is bought and which one is sold, value date, exchange rate, counterparty and settlement details if known.

The treasurer could also have said 'at 57' or 'mine'. All three ways would be correct and within market practice. Also, the dealer knew that the treasurer was used to market conventions and, hence, did not first quote the *big figure* of 123.

20.2.2   Example 2

Mr Jones is a high net worth individual who has a margin account with ABC International. He calls up and speaks to his favourite salesperson. After the customary pleasantries, Mr Jones asks for a dealing price for sterling in 'half a pound'. The salesperson obtains the price from the trader and communicates it to Mr Jones for consideration. It is likely that Mr Jones has a general idea of where the price is from his Internet screen. If Mr Jones accepts the price, the salesperson would immediately inform the trader, possibly via a hand signal. It is then up to the trader what happens with that position. The dealing conversation could be:

Mr Jones: A dealing price for half a pound please.
Corporate dealer: Sure, price for half a pound coming – Charlie (*trader*), cable in half?

Charlie: Who for?

Corporate dealer: Old Mr Jones.

Charlie: What's he doing?

Corporate dealer: How do I know – just give me the price.

Charlie: 30/40.

Corporate dealer: Cable in half a pound is 1.4330/40.

Mr Jones: Hmm, I was hoping for a better spread.

Corporate dealer: Your risk, let me try for you, you know it is only in half a pound but let me ask.

Charlie: What's he doing – trading or not?

Corporate dealer: He is looking for a better spread.

Charlie: What, in half a pound? You decide – he is your client.

Corporate dealer: I am 1.4332/37 now.

Mr Jones: Hmmm ... well ...

Corporate dealer: Mr Jones, your risk again.

Mr Jones: Ok, how now please?

Corporate dealer: Charlie – how are you left on that half pound for Mr Jones?

Charlie: Has he still not dealt – do what you like within 30/40 and let me know this side of Christmas.

Corporate dealer: 1.4333/38.

Mr Jones: Ok, I sell

Corporate dealer: Ok to confirm you sell half a million pounds and buy dollars at 1.4333 for value spot.

Mr Jones: Agreed and thanks.

20.3   A MATTER OF SECONDS

The process of the above two examples happens in only one or two seconds as markets move very rapidly. The salesperson and the trader can always change the price as long as the client has not firmly accepted the last quote made. Before making a decision to actually trade, it is not unusual for a client to shop around for quotes from various market makers in order to obtain the best deal. Sometimes, clients will ask for quotes knowing that they are not ready to actually trade but just want to check where the market is.

20.4   INFORMATION NEEDED

Hence, the following information is needed when asking for a quote:

- the two currencies being traded (for example, $/jpy);
- the value date of the trade (for example, spot);
- the amount (for example, $ 1 million).

If possible, the trader will try to know what side of the price you are, or at best guess. *Always ask for a two-way quote*.

20.5   FORWARD ASKING

Quotation of prices and dealing in the forward market are rather different from spot dealing. Theoretically, it is possible for the forward price of a currency to equal its spot price. However, because the interest rate that can be earned by holding different currencies usually varies, in practice the forward price is normally higher or lower than the spot rate. For convenience, forward prices are not quoted outright and instead dealers quote the differential (the premium or discount). The main benefit of quoting in this way is that the forward rates are subject to much less fluctuation than spot rates, so quoting in this way requires fewer changes to the price. For example, consider the following conversation:

Salesperson: Hello Mr Smith, how can I help you?
Mr Smith: Hi Susan, you know about 30 minutes ago I asked you for a 3-month forward price in dollar yen – is it still the same?
Salesperson: Let me just check for you, the spot has of course moved, but I am sure nothing has changed on the forward pips. Is it for the same amount you asked for before – 1 million dollars?
Mr Smith: Yes it is.
Salesperson: Yes, it is still the same. The price is 62 at 61.
Mr Smith: Ok, so at 62 I buy and sell 1 million dollars please.
Salesperson: Ok, so at 62 pips you buy and sell 1 million dollars and you sell and buy the yen; rates are 121.62 and 121.00, value dates being 23 March against 23 June. Anything else I can do for you?
Mr Smith: No thanks, all agreed and thanks, bye.

CONCLUDING REMARKS

In all cases, be extremely clear in the details of a trade or the instructions given, in order to avoid costly errors at a later stage. It is all too easy to mis-hear a quote 'for a half' and think it is a quote in 'four and a half'. Hence, the following two main principles should be followed:

- Always be concise – a phone trade is a binding contract, especially when transacting. Make perfectly clear which currency is being sold, which one is being bought and by whom ('I buy, you sell').
- Confirm amounts, currencies, rates and dates – Make it a habit of every trade to confirm every detail of a trade.

It is all too easy today to be over confident and some potentially very serious mistakes can occur, especially when the client wants one thing and the trader understands something very different. Common trading errors tend to occur when:

- trading on the wrong side – by and large a serious mistake, which can only be corrected by reversing the trade, that is buying or selling double the original amount.
- trading for the wrong amount – generally, the foreign exchange market trades in units of millions. The expression 'one euro' is understood to mean 'one million euros'. A 'yard' is slang for a billion units, especially used when trading the Japanese yen.
- quoting the wrong 'big figure' – can be serious and usually happens in fast moving markets where the price spans a couple of big figures.
- trading for a forward date that is incorrect – this could be due to a holiday in one of the currencies being quoted and is a minor error and easily corrected.
- using a premium instead of a discount or vice versa for forward trades – this can be corrected.

21
Foreign Exchange Market Orders

The previous chapter described the most frequent methods of foreign exchange dealings. However, a client may leave orders with the bank or broker, and there are generally four types of orders.

21.1 MARKET ORDERS

First, there are market orders, which enables the client to execute a transaction at the best available price immediately. No price is specified on the order. Since it is to be executed at the 'market', i.e. at the price prevailing when the order is actually done, the client is trying to establish or get out of a position as quickly as possible and, hence, timing is critical. For example:

Client: I want to sell 10 million Swiss francs value spot – what is your quote please?
Trader: I will buy 10 million Swiss francs and sell dollars at 1.6710 for value spot.

Spelling out, almost pedantically, the flow of funds will avoid problems at a later stage. If a client agrees to the way the trader expresses the deal, there should be no discrepancies. The quote is the price prevailing in the market.

21.2 AT BEST ORDERS

Second, there are 'at best orders'. This type of order enables the client to execute a transaction at the best available price. No price is specified on the order, which allows the bank to execute the order with little impact on the prevailing market conditions. This type of order is usually for 'large transactions'. A client trying to establish or get out of a position as quickly as possible uses at best orders. The client who does not want to disrupt the market also uses this type of order. However, take care with the terminology. For example:

Client: Sell 50 million dollars for me against the yen and let me know the price of this order once it has been executed. *Wrong!*

Client: I am a seller/I want to sell 50 million dollars and buy yen. Please let me know the price at which you have executed this order, later on. *Right!*

In the first conversation, there could be some confusion about who is buying, who is selling, and what currency. The trader will hear 'sell' and could assume that he or she is to be the seller of dollars.

21.3   STOP ORDERS

Third, there are stop orders. As the foreign exchange market can be volatile and currency values can change rapidly within a short period of time, stop orders are, therefore, used by clients to protect themselves against sudden price movements. These orders are used to limit losses, or to protect profits on previously established positions, or to initiate new positions when market moves occur. The important point to note about stop orders is that they are **contingent orders** and are only executed when the stop price has traded or is touched. The way the stop order works is that a market order would be triggered if and when the price reached the designated price. A **buy stop** order is placed above the market price, and if the market rises to the 'stop' level specified in the order, the order becomes a **market buy** order. A **sell stop** order is placed below the market order when the market drops to that level. In that event, it would be executed as a **market sell** order.

For example, assume that the client has previously bought 5 million Swiss francs against the dollar at 1.6710. The client wants to limit losses in the event that the market moves adversely. The client will, therefore, enter a sell stop at 1.6650. The client would then enter the order as:

Client: Stop loss sell 5 million Swiss francs against the dollar at 1.6650.

If the market drops to $/Sfr 1.6650, the trader will immediately execute the sell stop at the next *best available price*. Today, it is very rare for stop losses to be filled at the price.

21.4   DISCRETIONARY PRICE ORDER

The fourth type of order is a discretionary price order, which, in effect, is a stop order, but the client will establish at the outset the price at which he or she wants to deal but will give the trader the discretion to do better if possible than the stated price. If, in the attempt to do better, the trader misses the level because the market has moved suddenly, there can be no recriminations on the client's part. These orders are perhaps the most difficult to execute, since it puts a responsibility on the trader to do the best that can be done in sometimes difficult conditions for both parties.

CONCLUDING REMARKS

In all situations, whether dealing or leaving orders, please remember to make sure that all the instructions/details are clear and that the person on the other end of the phone (or Reuters, etc.) clearly repeats the instructions/details back to you.

Glossary of Terms for Chapter 21

The following lists the more popular orders used in both the foreign exchange and the futures market. Although the two markets share common orders, some are only relevant for the futures market, for example 'market on opening'. Hence, it is very important to state exactly and clearly what the order is and what, if necessary, you are trying to achieve.

Fill or kill (FOK)   This is used by clients wishing an immediate fill, but at a specified price. If the price is not attainable, the order is 'killed'.

Limit order   This is an order to buy or sell at a designated price. Limit orders to buy are placed below the market while limit orders to sell are placed above the market.

Market if touched (MIT)   This is the opposite of a stop order. A buy MIT is placed below the market and a sell MIT is placed above the market. It is normally used to enter the market or initiate a trade. It becomes a market order once the limit price is touched or passed through. An execution may be at, above or below the originally specified price.

Market on close   This order will be filled during the final seconds of trading at whatever price is available.

Market on opening   This is an order that the client wishes the trader to execute during the opening of trading at the best possible price obtainable within the opening range.

Market order   The market order is executed at the best possible price obtainable at the time the order reaches the trader.

One cancels the other (OCO)   This is a combination of two orders written on one order ticket. Once one side of the order is filled, the remaining side of the order should be cancelled. This type of order eliminates the possibility of a double fill by having both orders on one ticket.

Spread   The client wishes to take a simultaneous long and short position in an attempt to profit via the price differential or 'spread' between two prices.

Stop close only   The stop price on a stop close only will only be triggered if the market touches the stop during the close of trading.

Stop limit   This order lists two prices and is an attempt to gain more control over the price at which the stop is filled. The first part of the order is written like a stop order. The second part of the order specifies a limit price. This indicates that once the stop is triggered, you do not wish to be filled beyond the limit price.

Stop order   A buy stop order is placed above the market and a sell stop order is placed below the market. Once the price is touched, the order is treated like a market order and will be filled at the best possible price.

22
Electronic Foreign Exchange Trading

For the past few decades, the telephone has been the near universal means of communication between the banks and their clients for the executions of foreign exchange. The telephone has served the needs of the market well but now, with the advent of Internet trading, it is a moot point as to whether deal execution is significantly easier and more efficient using a computer instead of the telephone. Some would offer this as an argument against the introduction of e-commerce solutions to the foreign exchange markets. Some fear that a consequent reduction of personal contact between salesperson and client could undermine valued relationships.

22.1 DAYS GONE BY

Not so long ago, banking institutions were the sole purveyors of the information vital to the transaction of business in the market. With no central organized market, bank dealers executed trades solely by telephone or telex, writing trade details on pieces of paper, keeping positions on blotters and maintaining charts by hand. The resulting scarcity of information meant that price discovery was inefficient, bid–offer spreads were wide, margins were large, and major institutions played the largest role simply because they knew where activity and prices in the marketplace were occurring.

As a result, foreign exchange trading was a profitable activity for these institutions. The risks of trading were somewhat controlled and isolated at the bank level, with a degree of volatility sufficient enough to warrant active participation by only the most sophisticated of market participants.

22.2   THE ENVIRONMENT TODAY AND TOMORROW

Today, most clients are quite sophisticated; they know where the market is and what bid–offer spreads to expect for the foreign exchange deals. Banks and brokers who are uncompetitive in their pricing don't even leave the starting blocks in the race to win foreign exchange business. What distinguishes the best from the rest is the provision of high-quality information, in the way of charting and flows of relevant market information. In addition, clients are looking for systems that are Internet enabled, scalable across regions, reliable and safeguarded against crashes. Clients are also looking for Internet platforms, which offer real-time risk management systems, among other demands.

Access to price information is, today, widely available. Institutional investors and retail investors can now gain live access to multi-contributor price feeds, which can be downloaded directly into spreadsheets, if necessary. In addition, up-to-the-minute political and economic developments are widely available through news sources such as Bloomberg and CNBC. As a result of these developments, however, bid–offer spreads have collapsed, as have profit margins and this, in turn, has hampered the growth of direct investor participation.

According to recent research and surveys, the foreign exchange market is expecting electronic trading to account for approximately 80 % of the overall foreign exchange market by 2010 (eFX volumes currently account for roughly 62 % of the global foreign exchange market) with this rise being led by the rapid deployment of foreign exchange algorithms by investment managers seeking best execution across asset classes. Initiated by hedge funds searching for alpha and the demand for direct access through prime brokers to dealing desks at major global banks, asset managers are now bringing foreign exchange trading in-house. With this continued growth in electronic trading and the fragmentation of foreign exchange liquidity, foreign exchange algorithms will become standard fare on the desktops of both buy-side and sell-side traders.

22.2.1   Algorithmic Trading

Algorithmic trading has exploded in the foreign exchange market over the past couple of years, with traders now being able to supplement screen based trading with faster, smoother and more efficient automated dealing mechanisms. Foreign exchange is particularly suited to algorithmic trading because of the high levels of liquidity and the growing use of electronic trading. Driving the use of algorithmic trading strategies are hedge funds, high-frequency traders, proprietary traders and the rapid growth of foreign exchange futures trading at the Chicago Mercantile Exchange (CME).

Today, there is a certain amount of confusion as to what exactly constitutes an algorithmic trading solution. Indeed, the term has been used interchangeably with such terms as 'program trading' and 'black-box trading'. However, broadly defined, an algorithm is any quantitative model that automatically executes a specific order according to the parameters of the given algorithm and includes any user-defined constraints that can be imposed at the time of execution. Specifically, algorithms analyse an order and determine the timing, size and destination of its constituent trades. In many cases, they are designed to generate results tied to a specific benchmark.

Within the market, there are four basic types of algorithmic trading:

- Statistical – trading strategies that should make money over time based on analysis of historical time series data. These strategies generate trading requirements when they spot opportunities and operate at different frequencies, such as a few actions per day (low frequency) to thousands of actions per day (high frequency).
- Auto-hedging or position targeting – dynamic monitoring and management of risk levels that generates hedging orders to get a desired risk position, for example setting trading rules to reduce a position when the size reaches a certain threshold or to pass undesired risk into the market place.
- Algorithmic execution strategies – the objective is to best work a trade to fulfil the execution objective, such as minimize market impact or execute quickly.
- Direct market access – is the optimization of access and connectivity to multiple trading platforms. By assuming the market risk of executing with the venues directly, market participants may achieve improvements in speed and cost that yield the edge required to make their strategies profitable.

It should be noted that algorithmic trading is different to systematic trading, which is the use of computerized models for trading on the foreign exchange markets, for example trend following or carry models, whereas algorithmic trading is generally defined as computerized market making or execution models. In addition, it is generally recognized that systematic trading commonly involves taking speculative positions in the market, whilst algorithmic trading involves getting the best trade execution.

22.3   INTERNET REVOLUTION

The development of Internet-based trading has created a virtually zero-cost delivery channel. Information is now universal and market participants can distribute rates and price spreads 24 hours a day, 7 days a week to an unlimited number of potential market participants, ranging from the small-time retail player to the major league player. Thus, the Internet is transforming today's market through the low demands it makes on staff and technology. Using the Internet in foreign exchange investing means that there are no errors or transaction volume constraints. Also, active traders can exploit even the narrowest of margins, thus increasing the potential participation of the smallest retail client who is used to paying as much as 5 % to trade foreign exchange.

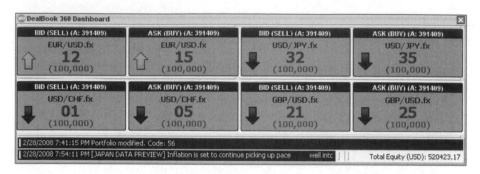

Figure 22.1 Click-'n'-deal. Reproduced by permission of GFT Global Markets. *Source:* GFT Global Markets – DealBook® 360

22.3.1 Internet Trading Platforms

There are three distinct types of Internet trading platforms, whether multibank portal, for example FXAlliance, or single portal, which are available for use by most market participants:

- **Click-'n'-deal** is the most common in the market and is, perhaps, the most transparent, in that the pricing is not 'marked' one way or another, as there is no trader intervention. The prices are live and instantly tradable by just clicking on a currency pair (Figure 22.1).
- **Request-for-price** uses a chat function for requesting the prices. This requires a trader to pick up the conversation and to physically type in the price. The downside to this system is that the pricing is not transparent as the trader has time to check a client's position before quoting a price. Thus, the trader has the ability to 'shade' the price one way or the other.
- Instant **anonymous** trading between principles allowing traders to see every bid and offer in the book and thereby greatly increases market transparency.

22.3.2 Choosing the Right Platform

In a market where competition and technological advances result in ever increasing product development from electronic foreign exchange trading platform providers, market participants are faced with a changing array of solutions. In such situations, it is initially important to focus on an inward analysis of the key objectives for online dealing before launching into platform selection. Only when these objectives are clearly understood, should market participants map their requirements against the functionalities of the various platforms.

The most important step in selecting a platform is in analysing some critical factors, such as comparing online dealing platforms and especially looking at their key differentiating factors. This can make the selection process appear bewildering but it is important to take into account such factors as:

- range of foreign exchange products;
- range of non foreign exchange products, including derivatives;
- dealing options – live pricing, quotes, orders, etc.;
- response times;
- foreign languages screen;
- geographic coverage;
- availability and quality of market research;
- financial strength;
- commitment to market;
- relationship approach;
- contractual approach.

22.4   WHAT ELSE TO EXPECT?

The majority of single portals not only offer a platform on which to trade, but also quite a lot more, and all in competition with each other. For example, looking at the IFXMarkets Ltd platform (www.ifxmarkets.com), IFX Direct not only offers real-time tradable prices in 20 spot currency pairs, but also IMM and Finex EFP contracts. To complement these live streaming prices, there is a 'chat' function, which allows all clients access to speak to the traders directly. In addition to this, their technology also offers a working order capability, which can create complex linked orders. Their on-line back-office system allows clients to check their open positions, equity and profit and loss status. IFX Direct also provides access to real-time charting, real-time news, market information and technical analysis.

CONCLUDING REMARKS

It can be seen from the above that the foreign exchange markets are no longer the domain of large traders with multimillion dollar accounts and connections at large banks. The electronic forex revolution is here and is providing traders of all sizes legitimate options for trading foreign exchange. eforex, or direct access trading of spot currencies, is now easier than ever and, like electronic trading of stocks, will be here to stay. It has the potential to revolutionize investment behaviour and provide more trading opportunities than ever before.

In addition, with this growth of Internet foreign exchange trading, the whole playing field has changed dramatically and electronic trading has certainly thrown

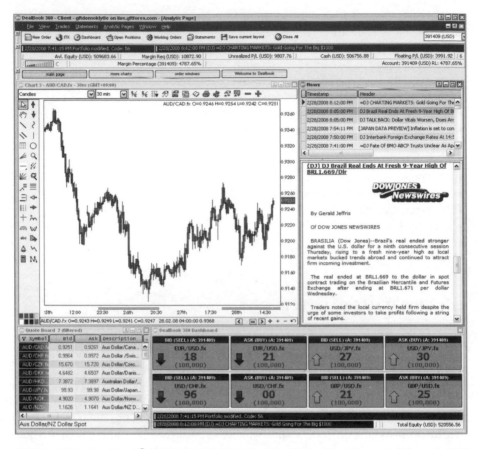

Figure 22.2 DealBook® 360 Real-time information. Reproduced by permission of GFT Global Markets. *Source:* GFT Global Markets – DealBook® 360

the cat among the pigeons where foreign exchange is concerned. It has already led to some remarkable changes within the market but it definitely has the potential to do even more and for the platform providers the challenge is to evolve even further in order to keep pace.

An average individual armed with a computer, a mouse and an Internet connection can trade spot foreign exchange literally 24 hours a day, 7 days a week. It seems that, overnight, an industry has sprung up to satisfy this market. Firms that did not exist one or two years ago are now growing rapidly. Such firms often provide free charts, signals, quotes, technical analysis, full simulation platforms and sometimes even financing to open an account. What was before the domain of the banks, corporations and funds is now accessible to everyone.

Just consider the leverage. eforex trading can boast levels far higher than futures and certainly equities. It's common for trading platforms to offer 50-to-1 and 100-to-1 leverage, enabling trading of $ 100 000 worth of a foreign currency with only 2 % or $ 2000 cash in the account.

While the Internet will play an increasing role in encouraging direct institutional and retail participation on the foreign exchange market, to date this has mainly been occurring through business-to-business solutions, notably proprietary electronic systems developed by banks that give clients access to their research and prices. However, the banks should be on their guard. Primary market makers, such as GFT Global Markets, should be viewed as real competitors for the day-to-day business that exists in the foreign exchange Internet market.

23
Margin Trading

Margin is borrowing money from a broker to buy a stock, or commodity, or currency pair and using the investment as collateral. It is, in effect, a performance bond in cash or another means of collateral deposited by a trader. Investors generally use margin to increase their purchasing power to enable them to own more stock or take larger positions in the market, without fully paying for it. However, margin exposes investors to the potential for higher losses.

The concept of 'trading on margin' is not new and has been employed by professional traders throughout the twentieth century. Over recent years, there has been a growing cadre of self-styled market experts who have been day trading and tend to be the main users of margin trading or 'leveraged' trading via newly created companies that provide trading facilities for such traders or those who rely on Internet connections to trading sites.

> **Margin is referred to as collateral, which implies leverage trading.**

23.1 UNDERSTAND HOW MARGIN WORKS

The easiest way to understand how margin actually works is to assume, for example, that a trader bought a stock for $ 50 and the price of the stock rises to $ 75. If the trader bought the stock in a cash account and paid for it in full, the trader would be able to earn a 50 % return on the investment. But, if the trader bought the stock on margin – paying $ 25 in cash and borrowing $ 25 from a broker – the trader will have 100 % return on the money invested and, of course, still owe the broker $ 25 plus interest.

The downside to using margin is that if the stock price decreases, substantial losses can mount quickly. For example, if the stock bought for $ 50 falls to $ 25 and the trader paid for the stock in full, the trader will lose 50 % of the money. However, if the trader bought on margin, he or she will lose 100 % and will still have to pay the interest owed on the loan.

In volatile markets, traders who put up an initial margin payment for a stock or currency position may, from time to time, be required to provide additional cash if the price of the stock falls. Some traders have been shocked to find out that the brokerage firm has the right to sell their securities that were bought on margin – without notification and potentially at a substantial loss to the trader. Thus, if the broker sells the trader's stock after the price has plummeted, then the trader will lose the chance to recoup the loss if the market regains.

In currency terms, when a trader buys (goes long) or sells (goes short) a currency pair, the value of the currency pair, as an instrument, is initially close to zero. This is because (in the case of a buy) the quote currency is sold to buy an equivalent amount of the base currency. As the market rates fluctuate, the value of the currency pair position held will also fluctuate. Thus, if the rate for the currency pair goes down, the trader's long position will lose value and become negative. To ensure that the trader can carry the risk in case a position results in a loss, a broker will typically require sufficient margin to cover those losses.

23.2   A SIMPLE EXAMPLE

If a client opens an account with $ 100 000, with an agreed margin level of 5 %, the client will be allowed to trade with 20 times leverage (100 divided by 5) which means that the client needs to maintain 5 % of any open position. Hence, the client can have open positions to the value of $ 2 000 000 ($ 100 000 divided by 5 %). As profit or losses occur, the amount that can be traded varies accordingly. Thus, if the client made a $ 20 000 profit one day, then he or she could have an open position of $ 2 400 000 ($ 100 000 + $ 20 000 = $ 120 000 divided by 5 %).

23.3   RECOGNIZE THE RISKS

Margin accounts can be very risky and are not suitable for everyone. Before opening a margin account, understand that:

- you can lose more money than you have invested;
- you may have to deposit additional cash or securities in your account on short notice to cover market losses;
- you may be forced to sell some or all of your securities when market prices reduce the value of your securities; and
- your brokerage firm may sell some or all of your securities without consulting you to recoup the loan it made to you.

In order to protect against any of the above, you should know how a margin account works and what happens if the price of the stock purchased on margin declines. You should also know that the firm charges interest for borrowing money and realize how that will affect the total return on the investment. Be sure to ask the broker if it makes sense to trade on margin in light of financial resources, investment objectives held and tolerance for risk.

23.4 GENERAL MARGIN RULES

In general, brokers will require a margin to be deposited with the firm before trading can begin. Today, margin rates vary from 1 % upwards, depending on the currency pair. For example, trading the euro against the dollar can be traded quite readily on just a 1 % margin, while taking a position in a more volatile currency pair, like the South African rand against the dollar, could require a margin of 25 %.

Obviously, in order to maintain a currency position, there must be sufficient funds to cover any potential loss:

- *Initial* margin represents the resources required to open a position.
- *Variation* margin represents the current profit or loss being made on any open positions.
- *Maintenance* margin is a minimum amount of collateral needed in the account.

23.5 MARGIN CALLS IN VOLATILE MARKETS

Many margin investors are familiar with the 'routine' margin call, where the broker asks for additional funds when the equity in the customer's account declines below certain required levels. Normally, the broker will allow from two to five days to meet the call. The broker's calls are usually based upon the value of the account at market close since various securities regulations require an end-of-day valuation of customer accounts.

However, in volatile markets, a broker may calculate the account value at the close and then continue to calculate calls on subsequent days on a real-time basis. When this happens, the investor might experience something similar to the following example with stocks:

Day 1 Close: A customer has 1000 shares of XYZ in the account. The closing price is $ 60, therefore, the market value of the account is $ 60 000. If the broker's equity requirement is 25 %, the customer must maintain $ 15 000 in equity in the account. If the client has an outstanding margin loan against the securities of $ 50 000, the client's equity will be $ 10 000 ($ 60 000 − $ 50 000 = $ 10 000). The broker determines the client should receive a margin call for $ 5000 ($ 15 000 − $ 10 000 = $ 5000).

Day 2: At some point early in the day there has been a 'dramatic' move in the market and the broker contacts the client to inform him that he has x number of days to deposit $ 5000 in the account. Shortly thereafter, on Day 2, the broker sells the customer out without notice.

What happened? In many cases, brokers have computer-generated programs that will issue an alarm (and/or take automatic action) if the equity in a customer's account further declines. For example, assume that the value of the XYZ stock in the customer's account continues to decline during the morning of Day 2 by another $ 6000 – that is, the shares are now worth only $ 54 000. The customer still has a loan outstanding to the broker of $ 50 000, but now the broker only has $ 54 000 in market value securing that loan. So, based upon the subsequent decline, the broker decided to sell shares of XYZ before they could decline even further in value.

Had the value of the securities stayed at about $ 60 000, the broker would probably have allowed the customer the stated number of days to meet the margin call. Only because the market continued to decline did the broker exercise its right to take further action and sell out the account.

CONCLUDING REMARKS

Margin-based trading refers to trading in transaction sizes larger than the funds in the account. By leveraging the funds in the account, traders can take better advantage of small movements in the market to build up profits quickly. Conversely, leveraging an account to trade in larger transaction sizes can just as easily work against a trader and magnify losses, essentially putting most of the funds in the account at risk. As trading foreign exchange on margin can be very rewarding, a strict trading discipline should be adhered to.

In order to limit the risks, a trader should continuously monitor the status of the positions against current market prices and should run stop-loss orders for each position open. A stop-loss order specifies that an open position (trade) should be closed automatically when the exchange rate for the currency pair in question reaches the specified threshold. For long positions, the stop-loss rate is always lower than the current market exchange rate, while for short positions, it is always higher.

Part IV
Fundamentals and
Technical Analysis

24
Fundamental versus Technical Approaches

The first factor to note about foreign exchange prices is that they are relative and not absolute.

> Foreign exchange prices are relative prices, not absolute prices.

They represent in the broadest sense a comparison of economies and all that this entails – for example, unemployment, inflation, wage performance, and budget balance. The extent to which one country performs better than another will be reflected in the relative value of its currency against the other's. Forecasting how a currency will move is still an art rather than a science. There are really two basic approaches, fundamental and technical, which need to be considered.

24.1 FUNDAMENTAL APPROACH

The **fundamental approach** relies on the analysis and understanding of several factors. Traditionally, currency forecasters look at economic factors, such as a country's balance of payments trend, to determine the direction of that country's currency exchange rate. The underlying theory is that a country cannot continue to run either a large trade deficit or a surplus without some consequent effect on its currency's exchange rate. This theory does not always hold true, as capital flows are becoming an important factor affecting exchange rates. Attention has, therefore, been given to both short- and long-term capital flows. From the balance of payments, the forecaster will look at the country's level of reserves, i.e. foreign exchange reserves including borrowing facilities, to determine the resources available to the central bank if the latter were to support a certain level of exchange rate. The fundamentalist will go

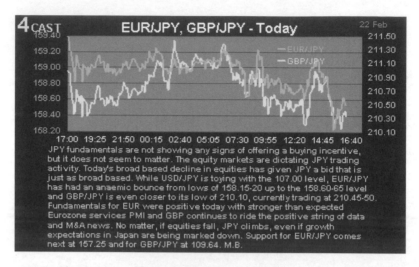

Figure 24.1 FX NOW! EUR/JPY, GBP/JPY Flows-JPY fundamentals soft, but still outperforms if equities slip. Reproduced by permission of 4CAST Limited. *Source:* 4castweb.com

through an analysis of the country's overall economic performance, i.e. domestic economy, as indicated by the gross domestic product. As statistics on the GDP are released on a quarterly basis, monthly data of key economic indicators like industrial production, personal income, industrial output, retail sales, and so on, will be closely monitored for clues to the exchange rate. Forecasters also believe that the higher a country's inflation rate relative to other countries, the faster will that country's currency depreciate. This is known as the purchasing power parity (PPP) theory (see Figure 24.1).

At times, a country's **social** and **political** environment also affects a country's exchange rate. Politics and politicians, their attitudes, affiliations and pronouncements are always closely scrutinized. For example, the results of a general election, a change of government or civilian unrest and consequent government actions have had, in the past, a marked impact on certain currencies. **Government** policy, which also must be considered as a factor, can be divided into two categories:

- First, **monetary policy** will encompass the level of interest rates, the growth of money supply, activities of the central bank in the domestic money market and in the foreign exchange market. The forecaster will attempt to gauge all of the above, especially interest rate levels, as they are a very important determinant of short-term capital flows. In fact, international investors look at relative interest rate levels to determine the currency in which to invest. Also, monetary authorities, by pursuing an expansionary policy to stimulate the economy, can attract long-term capital investments.
- The second category to note is the **fiscal policy** of a country.

However, there are political events that cannot be foreseen. The invasion of Kuwait in August 1990, the *coup d'état* of the Gorbachev government in August 1991, the NATO air strikes in Kosovo, or the terror attack on The World Trade Center in New York in September 2001. In such unforeseen events, a foreign exchange trader will initially respond by 'flight to quality' trades. In such circumstances, this usually means a move into either the dollar, the Swiss franc or gold.

24.1.1 Subjective Interpretation

The above are all factual considerations and can be observed by reading any reputable financial journal. However, it is the subjective interpretation of these elements that makes a market and causes some of the violent gyrations. The foreign exchange market is a dealing environment where the participants, for the most part, have at their disposal all the tools and information technology they need to make money. Most surround themselves with charts, Reuters and Telerate screens, and all have in-house economists to interpret economic trends. Thus, psychology, perceptions, expectations of future growth or political developments or what others expect (the safe haven concept), what has been and has not been discounted, and where the relative risks are or might be – all play their part (see Figure 24.2). Market operators look at all these factors when trying to anticipate where the next pressure point will be and to outguess the rest of the market.

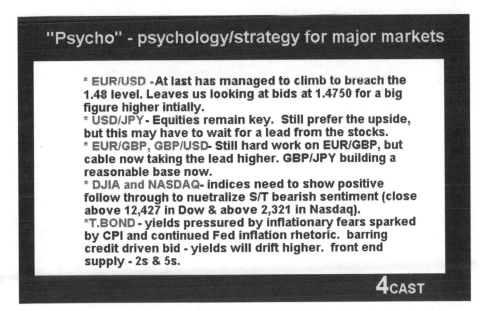

Figure 24.2 The psychology of major markets. Reproduced by permission of 4CAST Limited. *Source:* 4castweb.com

24.2   TECHNICAL APPROACH

The technical approach comprises two basic elements: **charting** and **technical analysis**.

- Charting involves the analysis of charts using various methods – for example, moving averages, reversal formations, point and figure charts, and trend line analysis.
- Technical analysis is the study and interpretation of price movements to determine future trends.

A technician will assume that all fundamental factors are reflected in the price and that history tends to repeat itself. The tools used by a technician are charts (bar, point and figure, line charts), mathematical models (moving averages, relative strength index, directional movement index), and behavioural models (Elliot wave theory and cycles) (see Figure 24.3).

24.3   CONCLUDING REMARKS

Economists have devised a wide range of theories to explain how exchange rates are determined, but the overwhelming body of evidence indicates that fundamental based

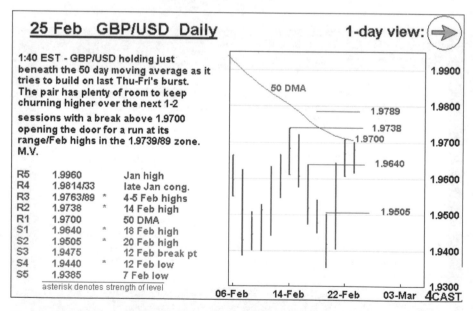

Figure 24.3   FX CHART GBP/USD Update: Pair challenging 50 DMA. Reproduced by permission of 4CAST Limited. *Source:* 4castweb.com

models, while useful in explaining longer-term trends in currency movements, have not met much success in explaining the short and medium-term trends that exchange rates take. Indeed, most studies suggest that at short- and medium-term horizons, a random walk characterizes exchange rate movements better than most conventional fundamental based exchange rate models. Exchange rates may move in the long run in the direction suggested by economic fundamentals, but the often chaotic behavior of exchange rates over short- and medium-term periods is capable of generating so much noise that it tends to obscure any discernible relationship between macroeconomic time series and the short- and medium-term movement of exchange rates.

However, many fund managers turn to technical analysis to help them formulate foreign exchange investment decisions, particularly over short-term horizons. Indeed a strong case can be made for using technical analysis over the short-term period since a variety of technical trading rules would have offered significant risk-adjusted profits had they been actively followed in the past. Unfortunately, total reliance on a technical-based approach to forecasting the foreign exchange markets can leave a trader vulnerable to frequent whipsaw losses caused by false technical signals.

Thus, participants in the foreign exchange markets base their decisions to buy or to sell foreign currencies on two types of analyses:

- Fundamental analysis, which is primarily the study of the relative economic, fiscal, monetary and political trends of the countries whose currencies are being traded. This type of analysis will lead to conclusions regarding relative investment values and currencies that may be bought and sold as a result.
- Technical analysis, where the philosophy states that price action itself embodies all information about the commodity and that trends and price behaviour can be analysed to make trading decision.

In reality, fundamental analysis of foreign exchange rates is a good background study, but a poor trading tool. On the other hand, technical analysis is a tactical tool used by speculators and traders, as the basis for position taking. At the end of the day, traders are usually uncomfortable about making an extensive foreign exchange bet on the basis of a technical recommendation if there is no fundamental view supporting the position taken. It would perhaps seem, therefore, that an ideal approach would be to combine the longer-run advantages of fundamental based models with the short-run advantages of technical based models.

25
Fundamental Analysis

Fundamentals focus on financial and economic theories, as well as on political developments to determine forces of supply and demand. In essence, fundamental analysis comprises the examination of macroeconomic indicators, asset markets and political considerations when evaluating a nation's currency in terms of another. Within this study, such figures as measured by Gross Domestic Product, interest rates, inflation, unemployment, money supply, foreign exchange reserves and productivity, are all considered.

Asset markets considerations comprise stocks, bonds and real estate, while political considerations impact the level of confidence in a nation's government, the climate of stability and level of certainty. Sometimes, governments stand in the way of market forces impacting their currencies and, hence, intervene to keep currencies from deviating markedly from undesired levels. Alternatively, some countries can manage to move their currencies merely by hinting or threatening to intervene.

25.1 PURCHASING POWER PARITY

The Purchasing Power Parity (PPP) theory states that exchange rates are determined by the relative prices of similar baskets of goods. Changes in inflation rates are expected to be offset by equal but opposite changes in the exchange rate. For example, if a bottle of Coke costs $2 in America and £1 in England, then, according to PPP, the pound–dollar exchange rate must be 2 dollars per 1 British pound. If the prevailing market exchange rate is $1.7 per British pound, then the pound is said to be undervalued and the dollar overvalued. The theory then assumes that the two currencies will eventually move towards the 2:1 relation. Therefore PPP's major weakness is that it assumes goods are easily tradable, with no costs to trade such as tariffs, quotas or taxes.

25.2   INTEREST RATE PARITY

This states that an appreciation or depreciation of one currency against another currency must be neutralized by a change in the interest rate differential. For example, if American interest rates exceed Japanese interest rates, then the American dollar should depreciate against the Japanese yen by an amount that prevents riskless arbitrage.

25.3   BALANCE OF PAYMENTS MODEL

This model holds that a foreign exchange rate must be at its equilibrium level, i.e. the rate that produces a stable current account balance. For example, a nation with a trade deficit will experience a reduction in its foreign exchange reserves, which ultimately lowers (depreciates) the value of its currency. The cheaper currency renders the nation's exports more affordable in the global marketplace while making imports more expensive. After an intermediate period, imports are forced down and exports rise, thus stabilizing the trade balance and the currency towards equilibrium.

Like PPP, the balance of payments model focuses largely on tradable goods and services, while ignoring the increasing role of global capital flows. In other words, money is not only chasing goods and services, but, to a larger extent, financial assets such as stocks and bonds.

25.4   ASSET MARKET MODEL

Economic variables such as growth, inflation and productivity are no longer the only drivers of foreign exchange movements. The proportion of foreign exchange transactions stemming from cross-border trading of financial assets has dwarfed the extent of currency transactions generated from trading in goods and services.

The asset market approach views currencies as asset prices traded in an efficient financial market. As a result, currencies are increasingly demonstrating a strong correlation with asset markets, particularly equities.

25.5   ECONOMIC INFLUENCES ON THE MARKET

As mentioned previously, currency forecasters traditionally look at the economic factors of a country to help them to determine the direction of a country's currency. Below is a more in depth analysis of the more important economic factors that have to be taken into consideration and cannot be ignored when announced.

25.5.1 Consumer Price Index

CPI is a measure of the average level of prices of a fixed market basket of goods and services purchased by consumers. The monthly reported changes in CPI are widely followed as an inflation indicator. The CPI often excludes the price of food and energy, as these items are generally much more volatile than the rest of the CPI and can obscure the more important underlying trend. Rising consumer price inflation is normally associated with the expectation of higher short-term interest rates and may therefore be supportive for a currency in the short term. However, a longer term inflation problem will eventually undermine confidence in the currency and weakness will follow.

25.5.2 Durable Goods Orders

This is a measure of the new orders placed with domestic manufacturers for immediate and future delivery of factory hard goods. Monthly percent changes reflect the rate of change of such orders. The levels of, and changes in, durable goods orders are widely followed as an indicator of factory sector momentum. More often than not, the indicator excludes defence and transport orders because these are generally much more volatile than the rest of the orders and can obscure the more important underlying trend. Rising orders are normally associated with stronger economic activity and can therefore lead to higher short-term interest rates, which are often supportive of the currency, at least in the short term.

25.5.3 Gross Domestic Product

GDP is the broadest measure of aggregate economic activity available. Reported quarterly, GDP growth is widely followed as the primary indicator of the strength of economic activity. It represents the total value of a country's production during the period and consists of the purchases of domestically produced goods and services by individuals, businesses, other countries and the Government. A high GDP figure is often associated with the expectations of higher interest rates, which is frequently positive for the currency, at least in the short term, unless expectations of increased inflation pressure is undermining confidence in the currency at the same time.

25.5.4 Housing Starts

This is a measure of the number of residential units on which construction has begun each month and is widely followed in order to assess the commitment of builders to new construction activity. High construction activity is usually associated with increased economic activity and confidence. It is therefore considered a harbinger of higher short-term interest rates and can be supportive of the currency in the short term.

25.5.5   Payroll/employment

This is a measure of the number of people being paid as employees by non-farm business establishments and units of government. A monthly change in payroll/ employment reflects the number of net new jobs created or lost during the month and changes are widely followed as an important indicator of the economic activity. Large increases in payroll/employment are seen as signs of strong economic activity. This could eventually lead to higher interest rates, which would be supportive of the currency, at least in the short term. If however, inflationary pressures are seen to be building, this may undermine the longer term confidence in the currency.

25.5.6   Producer Price Index

Producer Price Index (PPI) is a measure of the average level of prices of a fixed basket of goods received in primary markets by producers. The monthly reports are widely followed as an indication of commodity inflation. The PPI often excludes the food and energy components as these items are normally much more volatile than the rest of the PPI and can thus obscure the more important underlying trend. A rising PPI is normally expected to lead to higher consumer price inflation and thereby to potentially higher short-term interest rates, which in effect will have a short-term positive impact on the currency. However, significant inflationary pressure will often lead to an undermining of the confidence in the currency involved.

25.5.7   Retail Sales

These are a measure of the total receipts of retail stores. Monthly percentage changes reflect the rate of change of such sales and are widely followed as an indicator of consumer spending. They are generally followed less auto sales, because they are generally more volatile and can hence obscure the more important underlying trend. They are measured in nominal terms and include the effects of inflation. Rising retail sales are often associated with a strong economy and therefore an expectation of higher short-term interest rates is often supportive for the currency, at least in the short term.

25.5.8   Trade Balance

The trade balance is a measure of the difference between imports and exports of tangible goods and services, and is a major indicator of foreign exchange trends. Seen in isolation, measures of imports and exports are important indicators of overall economic activity in the economy. Typically, a nation that runs a substantial trade balance deficit has a weak currency due to the continued commercial selling of the currency. This can, however, be offset by financial investment flows for extended periods of time.

25.6   CONCLUDING REMARKS

The forces of supply and demand determine the value of currencies and there are, as mentioned before, two radically different methods of predicting where the forces of supply and demand are heading. The first method, fundamental analysis, focuses on macroeconomics. By studying economic reports and or political developments, fundamental analysts interpret changes in the underlying factors that cause foreign exchange rates to fluctuate. The other type of analysis, practised by technicians, primarily makes judgements based upon price data displayed on charts.

26
Key Factors Impacting Currencies

On certain occasions, foreign exchange rates immediately reflect changes in economic conditions, while, on other occasions, the market adjusts only after a period of delay. In general, foreign currency traders will tend to focus on released information that will have an impact on the market within a matter of hours; this means that they will not hold very long positions as the odds of an unpredicted development effecting exchange rates increases with time. Therefore, to minimize market risk, traders tend to enter and exit the market quickly, while looking for ideas that, if sound, will produce short-term profits.

The following is a guide to the essential fundamentals and practical factors impacting key foreign exchange rates against the dollar.

26.1 FACTORS AFFECTING THE YEN AGAINST THE DOLLAR

Asian markets and currencies generally move with the yen because Japan is the economic engine for the region. Economic problems, and/or political instability in particular countries, often affect Japanese companies and banks, which are heavily invested in the region, and therefore Asian instabilities undermine the yen. However, the major factors affecting the yen against the dollar are:

- *Ministry of Finance* (MoF). This is the single most important political and monetary institution and it will often make verbal intervention statements that are aimed at avoiding undesirable appreciation/depreciation of the yen.
- *Interest rates*. The overnight call rate is the key short-term interbank rate. The call rate is controlled by open market operations designed to manage liquidity. The Bank of Japan will use the call rate to signal monetary policy.

- *Japanese Government bonds* (JGBs). The Bank of Japan buys 10- and 20-year JGBs every month to inject liquidity into the monetary system. The yield on the benchmark 10-year JGB serves as the key indicator of long-term interest rate spread, or the difference between the 10-year JGB yield and those on the American 10-year treasury notes. For example, falling JGBs (rising JGB yields) will usually boost the yen and weigh on the dollar.
- *Economic Planning Agency* (EPA). This is a government agency that is responsible for formulating economic planning and coordinating economic policies, including employment, international trade and foreign exchange.
- *Ministry of International Trade and Industry* (MITI). This is a government institution principally aimed at defending international trade competitiveness of Japanese corporations.
- *Economic data*. The most important economic data from Japan are:
  1. Gross Domestic Product;
  2. Tankan Survey (quarterly sentiment and expectations survey);
  3. international trade;
  4. unemployment;
  5. industrial production;
  6. money supply.
- *Leading stock index* (NIKKEI-225). A reasonable decline in the yen usually lifts stocks of Japanese export companies, which tends to boost the overall stock index.
- *Cross-rate effect*. The cross-rate between the euro and the yen (eur/jpy) can have an effect on the currency. For example, a rising dollar against the yen could be the result of an appreciating euro against the yen, rather than as a direct result of a strengthening dollar.

An example of fundamentals affecting the yen could be:

> The dollar turned sharply higher on Friday, USD/JPY apparently leading the charge. Japanese vice Finance Minister Kuroda theorized overnight that 'massive' selling of yen would reverse the deflationary spiral in Japan, and help boost exports. There was some initial reaction to the comments, but it wasn't until the NY afternoon session that yen selling (in very thin market) really moved the dollar higher.

26.2   FACTORS AFFECTING THE SWISS FRANC AGAINST THE DOLLAR

The Swiss franc moves primarily on outside events and not necessarily on domestic economic news. The Swiss franc is the world's premier safe haven currency and will gain strength in the following situations:

- uncertainty over the euro;
- crisis in the Persian Gulf;
- turmoil in emerging markets (especially Russia and Europe).

As such crises are resolved, the Swiss franc will then tend to weaken. This safe-haven status stems from the fact that the SNB retains independence in preserving monetary stability and the neutrality of Switzerland's political position. However, other factors that should be taken into consideration are:

- *Swiss National Bank* (SNB). The Swiss central bank does not use a specific money market rate to control monetary conditions in the market. In effecting, it has maximum independence in setting monetary exchange rate policy. The officials of the SNB can affect the Swiss franc by making occasional remarks on liquidity or money supply.
- *Interest rates.* The SNB uses the discount rate to announce changes in monetary policy.
- *Economic data.* The most important economic data released out of Switzerland are:
  1. M3 – broadest in money supply;
  2. Consumer Price Index;
  3. unemployment;
  4. balance of payments;
  5. Gross Domestic Product;
  6. industrial production.
- *Cross-rate effect.* Such cross rates as the euro against the franc (EUR/CHF) or sterling against the franc (GBP/CHF) can affect the dollar against the franc exchange rate. For example, a rise in sterling against the franc, triggered by an interest rate hike in Britain, could extend the Swiss franc's weakness against other currencies.
- *Other possible factors.* Due to the proximity of Switzerland to Germany (Euro-zone), the franc has exhibited a considerably positive correlation with the euro. For example, a sudden move in the euro against the dollar, perhaps triggered by a major fundamental factor, is most likely to cause an equally sharp move in the dollar against the Swiss franc in the opposite direction.

An example of fundamentals affecting the Swiss franc could be:

> The fact that the Swiss GDP figures were delayed perhaps should have given clues as to how bad the figures were going to be. The state of the economy would suggest that those with safe haven money parked in the franc might want to step up the search for an alternative. The dollar against the Swiss franc was heading up ahead of the releases, though this might also be down to the American FTC clearing Nestlé's bid for Chef America.

26.3   FACTORS AFFECTING THE EURO AGAINST THE DOLLAR

As the euro establishes a track record, it should become widely held as a reserve currency. This will encourage European central banks and others with large dollar holdings to reallocate their foreign reserves, which could be a long-term positive factor for the euro. Also, as European banks are quite heavily exposed to emerging markets in Asia and Latin America, any turmoil in emerging markets could hurt the euro and thus hurt GDP.

The following factors should also be taken into consideration:

- *European Central Bank* (ECB). The ECB controls the monetary policy for all the countries that adopted the euro (Eurozone), and also has a primary objective of price stability.
- *Interest rates*. The ECB's refinancing rate is the key short-term interest rate to monitor.
- *10-year government bond*. This is another important driver of the exchange rate. The German 10-year Bund is normally used as the benchmark.
- *Economic data* (see Figure 26.1). The most important data come from Germany, being the largest economy, and the key data are:
  1. Gross Domestic Product;
  2. inflation;
  3. industrial production;
  4. unemployment;
  5. German IFO survey (indicator of business confidence);
  6. budget deficits of the individual member countries.

Euroland Economic Data 30 Sep

BST	CTY.	Indicator	For	4CAST	Unit	Mkt	Prev.
06:00	FI	Industrial output (Prelim)	Aug		% y/y	-	5.2
07:00	DE	Wholesale sales	Aug		% y/y	-	-0.8
08:00	IT	PPI	Aug	0.1	% y/y	0.3	0.1
08:30	NL	PPI	Aug		% y/y	-	-1.0
09:00	IT	Non-EU Trade balance	Aug	1150	EUR mn		1400
09:00	IT	EU Trade balance	Jul	-100	EUR mn		-456
11:00	EU	Harmonised CPI (Prelim)	Sep	2.1	% y/y	2.1	2.1

4CAST   More >>

Figure 26.1 Euroland economic data. Reproduced by permission of 4CAST Limited. *Source:* 4castweb.com

- *Cross-rate effect* (e.g. the euro against the yen). For example, the euro against the dollar could fall if there was some significant positive news from Japan, which will filter through a falling euro against the yen exchange rate.
- *Other indicators*. There is a strong negative correlation between the euro against the dollar and the dollar against the Swiss franc. In most cases, a spike (dip) in the euro/dollar exchange rate will be accompanied by a dip (spike) in the dollar/franc exchange rate. This mainly occurs because the Swiss economy is largely dependent on the Eurozone economies.
- *Political factors*. As with all exchange rates, the euro is susceptible to political instability, such as the coalition governments of Germany, Austria and Italy.

Examples of fundamentals affecting the euro can be:

The past week was broadly a week of two halves for the Eurozone interest rate markets with the first 3 days of the week, through to the end of the 11th September anniversary, seeing a sharp sell-off before a partial rebound Thursday/Friday. The catalyst for the early week falls were Mr. Duisenberg's comments (at the weekend EcoFin meeting) that 'we regard the present monetary stance, including interest rates, to be suitable for the present situation and the foreseeable future. We expect there will be no shortage of traders looking for EUR/USD buy levels in the early part of the week.'

Asia is taking little notice of Chancellor Schroeder's Social Democrats party extending its opinion polls lead over the Christian Democrats. The German Daily, *Die Welt*, reported that Schroeder's strong stance against war in Iraq boosted Social Democrats' lead in the opinion poll. With less than 10 days for a general election, the German daily reported that two opinion polls to be released later today showed the SPD leading 3 percentage points ahead of the opposition conservatives. Market continues to focus on US stocks and data releases later today.

26.4 FACTORS AFFECTING STERLING AGAINST THE DOLLAR

- *Bank of England* (BoE). In 1997, the British central bank obtained independence in setting monetary policy in order to deliver price stability, and this objective is set by the government's inflation target. Perhaps it is not so independent, as the BoE remains dependent upon having to meet the inflation target set by the Treasury.
- *Interest rates*. Minimum lending rate (base rate) is the main interest rate the market watches. The BoE will also set monetary policy through its daily market operations.
- *Gilts*. These are government gilt-edged securities. The market will look to the spread differential between the yield on the 10-year American treasury note and the yield on the 10-year gilt.
- *Treasury*. The Treasury sets the inflation target for the BoE, even though their role in setting monetary policy has diminished sharply since the BoE was given its independence in 1997.

- *Sterling and European membership.* Every time the Prime Minister in Britain makes references regarding Britain's possible membership into the single European currency, the foreign exchange market tends to react. In essence, if the British public were to vote in favour of joining, British interest rates would have to converge to the same levels as those in Europe and sterling would have to be depreciated.
- *Economic data.* The most important data items to watch are:
  1. unemployment;
  2. average earnings;
  3. retail sales;
  4. Producer Price Index;
  5. industrial production;
  6. Gross Domestic Product growth;
  7. purchasing managers' surveys;
  8. money supply;
  9. housing prices.
- *Leading stock index* (FTSE-100). There is a correlation between the FTSE-100 and the Dow Jones Industrial Index which happens to be one of the strongest in the global markets.
- *Cross-rate effect.* Since sterling is outside the Eurozone, it is a popular safe haven from euro doubts. The key rate to watch is the euro against sterling cross (EUR/GBP) for the euro situation as well as other safe-haven plays. Also, if there were a strengthening of the possibility of British membership into the euro, this would lead to a rise in the euro against the pound and would lead to a decline in the pound against the dollar. Conversely, reports that Britain may not join the single currency will hurt the euro against the pound, thereby boosting sterling.

An example of fundamentals affecting sterling is:

> While the traders are focusing on the frenetic activity in EUR/JPY that has set off stops just over 118.20 and jumped to 118.41; GBP/JPY has benefited just as much from JPY weakness. From a fundamental perspective, GBP looks like an even better buy vs JPY due to the relatively good condition of the UK economy vs Euroland. Longer term investors have pushed GBP/JPY to 188.30, the highest price since the end of July. Dealers say that if the day's high of 188.42 is breached, the target on the upside is 189.90 which has not been seen since mid April. (*Source:* 4castweb.com)

26.5   FACTORS AFFECTING THE AMERICAN DOLLAR

- *Federal Reserve Bank* (Fed). The American central bank has full independence in setting monetary policy. Its chief policy signals are open market operations, the discount rate and the Fed Funds rate.
- *Federal Open Market Committee* (FOMC). This committee is responsible for making decisions on monetary policy, including the crucial interest rate announcements it makes eight times a year.

- *Fed Funds rate*. This is clearly the most important of all American interest rates. It is the rate that depository institutions charge for overnight loans. The Fed will announce changes in the rate when it wishes to send clear monetary signals to the market, and these announcements will generally have a major impact on all stock, bond and currency markets.
- *Discount rate*. This is the interest rate at which the Fed charges commercial banks for emergency liquidity, and is mostly a symbolic rate. However, changes in the discount rate imply clear policy signals.
- *30-year Treasury bond*. This is perhaps the most important indicator of the market's expectations on inflation. Being a benchmark asset-class, the long bond is normally impacted by shifting capital flows triggered by various considerations. Financial and political turmoil in emerging markets could be a possible booster for US treasuries for their safe nature, thereby helping the dollar.
- *10-year Treasury note*. The foreign exchange markets usually refer to the 10-year note when comparing its yield with that of bonds overseas. A higher American yield usually benefits the dollar against foreign currencies.
- *Treasury*. The Treasury is responsible for issuing government debt and for making decisions on the budget. The Treasury has no say in monetary policy but statements on the dollar have quite an influence on the currency.
- *Economic data* (see Figures 26.2 and 26.3). The most important release are:
  1. Labour report (payrolls, unemployment rate and average hourly earnings);
  2. Consumer Price Index;
  3. Producer Price Index;
  4. Gross Domestic Product;

US Economic Data 30 Sep

BST	Indicator	For	4CAST	Unit	Mkt	Prev.
13:30	Personal income	Aug	0.4	% m/m	0.6	0.0
13:30	Personal spending	Aug	0.5	% m/m	0.5	1.0
15:00	Chicago Purch. Index	Sep	52.0	index	52.0	54.9

4CAST   More >>

Figure 26.2 US economic data. Reproduced by permission of 4CAST Limited. *Source:* 4castweb.com

Global Economic Data 30 Sep

BST	CTY.	Indicator	For	4CAST	Unit	Mkt	Prev.
00:50	JP	Industrial production (Prelim)	Aug	3.0	% m/m	2.3	0.1
02:30	AU	Balance of goods and services	Aug	-1000	A$ mn	-900	-643
06:00	JP	Construction orders	Aug		% y/y	-5.6	-5.2
06:00	JP	Housing starts	Aug		% y/y	-3.0	-6.7
08:30	SE	Consumer confidence	Sep	8.0	points	-	9.1
11:30	NO	Unemployment	Sep	3.3	% rate	-	3.5
13:30	CA	GDP	Jul	0.4	% m/m	0.3	0.1

4CAST

Figure 26.3 Global economic data. Reproduced by permission of 4CAST Limited. *Source:* 4castweb.com

     5. International trade;
     6. NAPM;
     7. Housing starts and housing permits;
     8. Industrial production;
     9. Consumer confidence.

- *Stock market.* There are three major stock indexes: the Dow Jones Industrials Index (Dow), S&P 500 and NASDAQ. The Dow is the most influential index on the dollar. The three main forces affecting the indexes are corporate earnings (forecast and actual), interest rate expectations, and global considerations.
- *Cross-rate effect.* The dollar's value against one currency is sometimes impacted by another currency that may not involve the dollar. For example, a sharp rise in the yen against the euro could cause a general decline in the euro, including a fall in the euro against the dollar.

Some examples of the dollar being affected by fundamental factors could be:

The week centered on the first anniversary of the September 11th terrorist attacks on the US, with the days prior to Wednesday characterised by further reduction of risk, which in FX terms meant trimming back short USD positions. The day itself saw a gentle exploration of long USD positioning which appeared based on little more than an outbreak of patriotism, but while the USD rally did have more legs than that in the stock markets, the approach of Fed Chairman Greenspan's testimony to the House Budget Committee, President Bush's speech to the United Nations (both Thursday) and

US retail sales data followed by the Michigan CSI (Friday) ensured that risk profiles remained low. Mr Greenspan walked the usual center line, though did concede that the Fed's July forecasts on the US economy 'would somewhat lower' if re-estimated today. The retail sales data was better than expected, the Michigan was worse.

On the Iraq front, UN developments next week may ultimately determine the greenback's medium term direction, so USD gains posted today may be fleeting. A busy week on the data calendar next week brings July business inventories on Monday, August industrial production/capacity utilization on Tuesday. August CPI is on tap Wednesday, along with the July trade report and August real earnings. On Thursday, August housing starts and the September Philly Fed survey will be released. (*Source:* MMS)

27
Technical Analysis

In an earlier chapter, it has been mentioned that the technical approach comprises two elements, charting and technical analysis, which is the study and interpretation of price movements in order to determine future trends. A technician assumes that all fundamental factors are reflected in the price and that history tends to repeat itself. The tools of a technician are bar charts, point and figure charts, and line charts. Technicians will use mathematical models, such as moving averages, relative strength index (RSI) and directional movement index (DMI), and will also study behavioural models, such as Elliot Wave theory and cycles.

> Technical analysis examines past price and volume data to forecast future price movements.

27.1 ASSUMPTIONS

All technical analysis is based upon the following three assumptions.

1. All publicly available information about a tradable currency is already in its price.
2. Prices move in trends or patterns.
3. History repeats itself.

Thus, as a direct consequence of the first assumption, technicians believe there is little profit to be gained by researching economic fundamentals. This research will lead to an explanation of the current price rather than an accurate prediction of the future price. Hence, technicians look at charts to identify patterns and trends. They have found that currency prices do not fluctuate randomly, like the chaotic scrawl of a small child, but instead follow distinct patterns, like the crest and peaks of waves. By trying to identify known patterns or discernible trends in the early stages of their development, technicians predict rate movement based upon the historical continuations of those movements.

Technicians ignore statements by politicians and government officials. If the statement is important, it will be reflected in the foreign exchange rate. For example, if Ben Bernanke, the head of the American Federal Reserve (central bank) said that the American Federal Reserve would cut interest rate in the near future, fundamental analysts would immediately buy Swiss francs, euros and yen in exchange for dollars. This is because a lowering of American interest rates (or an increase in its probability) would make the dollar a less attractive investment compared to other currencies. The selling of dollars by traders who follow fundamentals would trigger a downward movement in the dollar against other currencies.

The technicians who were watching charts while Bernanke spoke would notice a plunge in the dollar on the charts. As different exchange rates began new trends, technicians would change their foreign exchange positions in the market. In this scenario, the technicians follow the lead of the fundamental analysts.

Technicians follow trends – they do not start market movements.

Fundamental analysts have the ability to follow a limited number of topics at one time. If a technician is occupied listening to Bernanke giving a speech, it is not usually possible to follow the events that are going on in Germany or Latin America. Thus, the technician indirectly through price movements may have a more complete perspective of all the unfolding activity than a fundamentalist.

27.2   THE BASIC THEORIES

The **Dow theory** is the oldest theory in technical analysis and states that prices fully reflect all existing information. This theory was developed primarily around stock market averages and holds that prices progressed into wave patterns which consisted of three types of magnitude: primary, secondary and minor. The time involved ranged from less than three weeks to over a year. The theory also identified retracement patterns, which are common levels by which trends pare their moves. Such retracements are 33 %, 50 % and 66 %.

27.2.1   Fibonacci Retracement

This is a popular series based on mathematical ratios arising from natural and artificial phenomena. It is used to determine how far a price has rebounded or backtracked from its underlying trend. The most important retracement levels are 38.2 %, 50 % and 61.8 %.

27.2.2   Elliot Wave

With Elliot Wave, technicians classify price movements in patterned waves that can indicate future targets and reversals. Waves moving with the trend are called **impulse waves**, whereas those moving against the trend are called **corrective waves**. The Elliot Wave theory actually breaks down impulse waves and corrective waves into five and three primary movements, respectively. The eight movements comprise a complete wave cycle. Time frames can range from 15 minutes to decades.

The challenging part of Elliot Wave theory is figuring out the relativity of the wave structure. A corrective wave, for example, could be composed of subimpulsive and corrective waves. It is, therefore, crucial to determine the role of a wave in relation to the greater wave structure. Thus, the key to Elliot Waves is to be able to identify the wave context in question. Followers also use Fibonacci retracements to predict the tops and bottoms of future waves.

27.3   WHAT TO LOOK FOR

1. *Find the trend.* Finding the prevailing trend will assist in becoming aware of the overall market direction and offer better visibility, especially when shorter term movements tend to clutter the picture. Weekly and monthly charts are most ideally suited for identifying that longer term trend. Once the overall trend has been identified, buy on the dips during rising trends, and sell the rallies during downward trends.
2. *Support and resistance.* These levels are points where a chart experiences recurring upward or downward pressure. A support level is usually the low point in any chart pattern, whereas a resistance level is the high or the peak of the pattern. These points show a tendency to reappear. It is best to buy near support levels and sell near resistance levels that are unlikely to be broken. Once these levels are broken, they tend to become the opposite obstacle. For example, in a rising market, a resistance level that is broken, could serve as a support for the upward trend, while, in a falling market, once a support level is broken, it could turn into a resistance.
3. *Lines and channels.* Trend lines are helpful tools in confirming the direction of a market trend. An upward straight line is drawn by connecting at least two successive lows, with the second point higher than the first. The continuation of the line helps to determine the path along which the market will move. An upward trend is a concrete method by which to identify support lines/levels. Conversely, downward lines are charted by connecting two points or more. A channel is defined as the price path drawn by two parallel trend lines. The lines serve as an upward,

downward or straight corridor for the price. A familiar property of a channel for a connecting point of a trend line is to lie between the two connecting points of its opposite line.

4. *Averages*. Moving averages tell the average price in a given point of time over a defined period of time. However, a weakness of moving averages is that they lag the market, so they do not necessarily signal a change in trends. To address this problem, the use of a shorter period, such as a 5- or 10-day moving average, would be more reflective of the recent price action than a 40- or 200-day moving average.

27.4   DRAWING LINES

It is easy to draw a chart by drawing a straight line joining two points, which usually means joining the high and the low of the day. In reading a chart, analysts will initially look for trend lines, where an **uptrend** is identified as a higher high and higher low, day after day, and a **downtrend** is a lower high and lower low, day after day. Secondly, they will look for a **consolidation** pattern, where the chart is characterized by inconsistent highs and lows. Finally, they will look for support and resistance areas, which are valid for both uptrends and downtrends (see Figure 27.1).

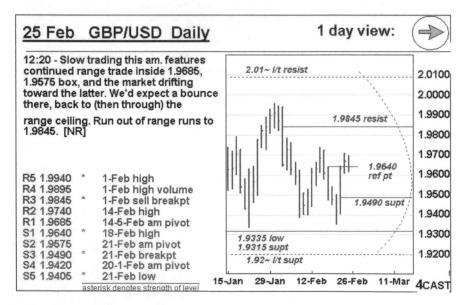

Figure 27.1   Support and resistance lines. Reproduced by permission of 4CAST Limited. *Source:* 4castweb.com

> **A support is a line joining all the bottoms and resistance is a line joining all the tops.**

27.5   HEAD-AND-SHOULDERS FORMATION

The most significant reversal formation is the head-and-shoulders formation, which can be a top head-and-shoulders or a bottom head-and-shoulders. Generally, this pattern is most often seen in uptrends. To have a head-and-shoulders formation, there has to be five points, as shown in Figure 27.2.

A rally to a top to form a left shoulder (point 1) followed by a correction (point 2), a second rally to form the head (point 3), followed by a correction to somewhere at the same level of point 2 to form point 4. This is then followed by a last rally to point 5 or the right shoulder. The height of the right shoulder should not be above the head. Once the right shoulder starts to decline, the chartist will start to identify a head-and-shoulders formation. The ideal head-and-shoulders formation has symmetry between the two shoulders and a near horizontal neckline. The neckline will be obtained by joining points 2 and 4.

A head-and-shoulders formation tells the analyst that there is a major change in trend. Once the price levels break the neckline, the chartist will expect the price to move to an objective determined by the distance from the top of the head to the

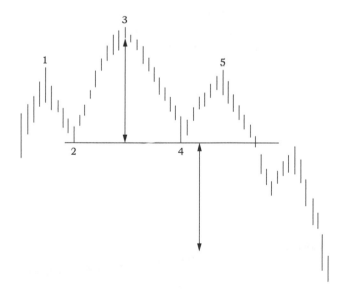

Figure 27.2   A head-and-shoulders formation

neckline, measured from the break of the neckline. Because this is such a major formation, one should expect the price to pull back towards the neckline, before resuming the new trend.

The above formations can sometimes be inverted, and is typically seen in down-trends. What is noteworthy about the inverted head-and-shoulders is the volume aspect. Normally, the inverted left shoulder should be accompanied by an increase in volume. The inverted head should be made on lighter volume. The rally from the head, however, should show greater volume than the rally from the left shoulder.

Ultimately, the inverted right shoulder should register the lightest volume of all. Finally, when the currency then rallies through the neckline, a large increase in volume should be seen.

27.6 FORMATION PATTERNS

27.6.1 The Symmetrical Triangle

Another formation or pattern is a symmetrical triangle formation, which must have four reversals of minor trend, as there has to be two top points and two bottom points in order to draw the two straight lines forming the triangle. In fact, symmetrical triangles can be characterized as areas of indecision. A market pauses and future direction is questioned. Typically, the forces of supply and demand at that moment are considered to be almost equal.

Prices may break out of a symmetrical triangle either up or down. It is important to wait until the breakout has started, as it is very difficult to determine the direction in which the breakout will occur. Once the breakout is confirmed, the price movement is requested to have an objective equal to the height of the triangle measured from point 2 (Figure 27.3).

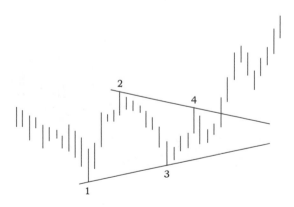

Figure 27.3 A symmetrical triangle formation

27.6.2 The Descending Triangle

This formation is also a variation of the symmetrical triangle. It is generally considered to be bearish and is usually found in downtrends. Unlike the ascending triangle, the bottom part of this triangle appears flat. The top part triangle has a downward slant. Prices drop to a point where they are oversold. Tentative buying comes in at the lows, and prices pick up. The higher price, however, attracts more sellers and process retests the old lows. Buyers then once again tentatively re-enter the market. The better prices, however, again attract even more selling.

Thus, sellers are in control and push through the old lows, while the previous buyers rush to dump their positions.

27.6.3 The Right-Angle Triangle

Two other formations of importance are a right-angle triangle, which can either be ascending or descending and is, respectively, a bullish or bearish sign. The ascending right-angle triangle is shown in Figure 27.4. It is a variation on the symmetrical triangle. Ascending triangles are generally most reliable when found in un uptrend. The top part of the triangle appears flat, while the bottom part of the triangle has an upward slant.

27.6.4 The Wedge

The wedge formation is also similar to a symmetrical triangle in appearance, in that it has converging trend lines that come together at an apex. However, wedges are distinguished by a noticeable slant, either to the upside or to the downside. A falling wedge is generally considered bullish and is usually found in uptrends. This pattern

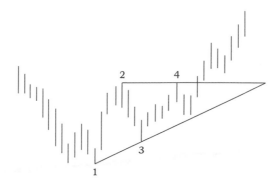

Figure 27.4 A right-angle triangle formation

is marked by a series of lower tops and lower bottoms. On the other hand, a rising wedge is generally considered bearish and is usually found in downtrends. They can also be found in uptrends, but would still generally be regarded as bearish. Rising wedges put in a series of higher tops and higher bottoms.

27.6.5   The Channel

Generally, channel formations should be considered as continuation patterns. They are indecision areas that are usually resolved in the direction of the trend and the trend lines run parallel in a rectangle. Supply and demand appears evenly balanced with buyers and sellers equally matched. The same highs are constantly tested, as are the same lows. With this formation, volume does not seem to suffer as it might do with other patterns. However, like other chart formations, volume in the market should noticeably increase on a breakout.

27.6.6   Flags and Pennants

Flags and pennants are small consolidations in trend lines and appear to be 'breathing spaces' before the trend continues. A flag in an uptrend is shown in Figure 27.5.

Flags and pennants can be categorized as continuation patterns as they usually represent only brief pauses in a dynamic currency. They are typically seen immediately after a large, quick move. The currency then usually takes off again in the same direction. Past experience has shown that these formations are some of the most reliable continuation patterns. In general, lower tops and lower bottoms characterize

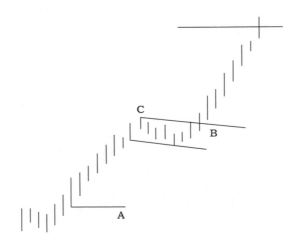

Figure 27.5   Flags and pennants formation

bullish flags, with the formation slanting against the trend. However, unlike wedges, their trend lines run parallel. On the other hand, bearish flags comprise higher tops and higher bottoms. The trend lines of bear flags run parallel, but also have a tendency to slope against the trend.

27.7   EXAMPLES

'Reaction/consolidation seen soon, but higher again to follow'

> 4Cast M/T View – USD/JPY – Tuesday 24 September 2002 Recovery from 115 nearing stronger resistance, but clearance over the next 2–3 months now seen more likely. (Ref. rate 123.25)

> Over the past month USD has been rallying above 115.00, the bottom of the 2001 range. This is now nearing an area of stronger resistance, and a reaction and consolidation of gains is therefore likely over the next few weeks. However, the extent of the recovery, which has cut initial downtrends, suggests that a significant low can already be in place. We would therefore now expect renewed gains to follow into the latter half of the next 2–3 months, confirmed above 126.00/127.00 resistance. (*See Figure 27.6.*)

> While rates are still firm in a shorter-term up trend, resistance is now close at hand towards the upper end of previous congestion at 125.80/90, the June peak area. Just above is 126.36/77, the March and early May lows and the beginning of the December/May top. This is not seen cleared without more consolidation, but a breakup is now anticipated

Figure 27.6   Reproduced by permission of 4CAST Limited. *Source:* 4castweb.com

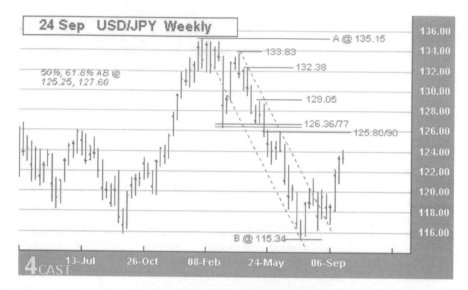

Figure 27.7 Reproduced by permission of 4CAST Limited. *Source:* 4castweb.com

after this. Look then for a move to 129.05, 9 May high. Above here would signal scope to challenge 132.38, 13 April high, and 133.83, 1 April high. Beyond is the 135.00/15 January/February peak area, then 140.00 historic congestion. (*See Figure 27.7.*)

Meanwhile support during the expected consolidation phase is now at 120.86, 19 September low, ahead of 120.00/119.40, congestion and the 13 Sep low. If this holds, an earlier resumption of gains will be in focus. More likely is a deeper reaction into the stronger congestion down to 116.80/26, 3

September and 14 August lows. These should hold. Failure, not currently anticipated, would retest 115.34, 16 July low. Clearance of this, now seen unlikely, would be needed to reinstate scope for a longer downswing, targeting next 110.00, the top of the large 1999/2000 base. (Beneath is 105.00, the mid area; this is the maximum downside seen and should hold any test.) (*See Figure 27.8.*)

In the next few weeks we expect the dollar's rally to give way to a reaction and consolidation phase. However, a more extensive retracement of the 2000/02 gains below 115.00 is no longer seen as likely. We rather expect higher support levels to hold, and be followed by renewed gains into the second half of the quarter. (*See Figure 27.9.*)

27.8 TECHNICAL INDICATORS

Below is the description of some of the most popular technical indicators used in the analysis of charts in the foreign exchange market today.

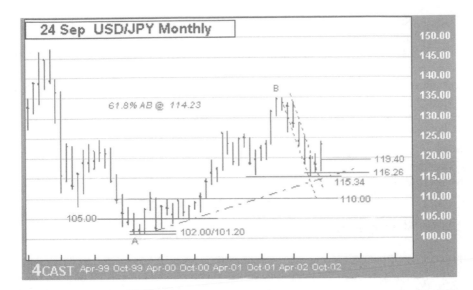

Figure 27.8 Reproduced by permission of 4CAST Limited. *Source:* 4castweb.com

Figure 27.9 Reproduced by permission of 4CAST Limited. *Source:* 4castweb.com

27.8.1   Relative Strength Index

RSI is a momentum indicator, which measures a currency's price relative to itself. It
is past performance and is also front weighted. This means it gives a better velocity
reading than other indicators. RSI is also less affected by sharp rises or drops in a
currency pair's performance. The RSI absolute levels are 1 and 100. Traditionally,
buy signals are triggered at 30 and sell signals are triggered at 70. However, today,
many seasoned campaigners are using 20 and 80 as the relevant buy and sell signals.
In effect, the RSI is like a rubber band, in that it can be stretched just so far. After a
certain point, unless it breaks, the band is forced to contract. It is also an indicator,
which lends itself to trend lines, support and resistance lines and divergence.

27.8.2   Moving Average

This is one of the oldest and most useful of the technical indicators. In its simplest
form, a moving average is the average price of a currency at a specific point in time.
Hence, it shows a trend and the purpose is to show the trend in a smoothed fashion. A
user will specify the time span, with the most common time period being 10-, 30-, 50-,
100- and 200-day moving averages. There really is not just one 'right' time frame.
Each technician will have his or her own favourite. It should be noted that moving
averages with different time spans will tell a different story, in that the shorter the
time span, the more sensitive the moving average will be to price changes. The longer
the time span, the less sensitive or the more smoothed the moving average will be.

27.8.3   Bollinger Bands

These are envelopes which surround the price bars on a chart. They are plotted two
standard deviations away from a simple moving average. The envelopes are plotted
at a fixed percentage above and below a moving average. Because the standard
deviation is a measure of volatility, the Bollinger Bands adjust themselves to the
market conditions. In fact, they widen during volatile market periods and contract
during less volatile periods. Sometimes, Bollinger Bands are displayed with a third
line, which is the simple moving average line. The time period for this moving
average can vary, but it is recognized in the market as 10 days for short-term trading,
20 days for intermediate term trading, and 50 days for longer term trading. Please
note, however, that Bollinger Bands do not generate buy and sell signals alone. In
theory, they should be used in conjunction with RSI or MACD (see below).

27.8.4   Moving Average Convergence Divergence

MACD is an oscillator, which is derived by dividing one moving average by another. With the capabilities of modern computers, the moving averages are usually

exponentially weighted, thus giving more weight to the more recent data. The MACD is plotted in a chart with a horizontal equilibrium line. This line is quite important, because when the two moving averages cross below the equilibrium line, it implies that the shorter EMA is at a value less than the longer EMA. This is a bearish signal. When the EMAs are above the equilibrium line, it implies that the shorter EMA has a value greater than the longer EMA, and is thus a bullish signal.

27.8.5   Stochastics

Oscillator compares where a currency's price has closed relative to its price range over a specifically identified period of time. The theory is that in an upward trending market, prices tend to close near their high, while in a downward trending market, prices tend to close near their low. Also, as an upward trend matures, price tends to close further away from its high, and as a downward trend matures, price tends to close away from its low. This indicator attempts to determine when prices start to cluster around their low of the day for an uptrending market and when the trend to cluster around their high in a downtrending market. Thus, these are the conditions that indicate a trend reversal is starting to occur.

CONCLUDING REMARKS

Technical analysis is an art in which quasi-statistical techniques and formal statistics are used to determine the existence and strength of trends in financial time series and to identify turning points in these trends. It is concerned with the 'when' and the 'how' of trading foreign exchange. It determines the optimal timing for a position, and its conclusions about how long to stay in a particular trade have significant importance. The market loves to announce, 'the trend is your friend', but timing is everything.

Glossary of Terms
for Chapters 24 to 27

Activity   Economic effect.

Consumer Price Index rises   Indicates rising inflation.

Durable Goods Orders rises   Pick up in business activity usually leads to increased credit demand.

Fed buys bills   Fed permanently adds to banking system reserves, which may cause interest rates to drop.

Fed does repurchase agreements   Fed puts money into the banking system by purchasing collateral and agreeing to resell later. This helps bring down rates.

Fed does reverses of matched sales   Fed takes money from the system by selling collateral and agreeing to repurchase them at a later date. This decrease in money supply generally raises interest rates.

Fed raises discount rate   An increase in the borrowing rate for banks from the Fed usually results in increased rates for clients of banks. This action is used to slow credit expansion.

Gross National Product falls   Reflects a slowing economy. Fed may loosen money supply, prompting a decline in interest rates.

Housing Starts rises   Shows growth in the economy and increased credit demand. Fed less accommodating and may attempt a tightening by allowing rates to rise.

Industrial production falls   Indicates slowing economic growth. Fed may be more accommodating in allowing interest rates to fall to stimulate the economy.

Inventories up   Indicates a slowing economy since sales are not keeping up with production.

Leading indicators up   Signals strength in the economy leading to greater credit demand.

Money supply increases   Excess money supply growth potentially can cause inflation and generate fears the Fed may tighten money growth by allowing the Fed Funds rate to rise, which in turn, lowers futures prices.

Oil prices fall   Reduces upward pressure on interest rates, thereby enhancing prices of debt securities.

Personal income rises   The higher one's income, the more is consumed, prompting increased demand and higher prices for consumer goods.

Precious metal price falls   Reflects decreased inflation. Demand for inflation hedges abates.

Producer Price Index rises   Indicates rising inflation. Demand for goods rises as well as prices. Investors require higher rates, pushing rates up.

Retail sales rises   Indicates stronger economic growth. Fed may have to tighten.

Unemployment rises   Indicates slow economic growth. Fed may ease credit, causing rates to drop.

28
Market Psychology

___

28.1 PSYCHOLOGY OF TRADING

28.1.1 Introduction

None of us are born traders, successful or otherwise, and there is a harsh recognition that the vast majority of all traders who lose are not psychologically prepared to trade. In effect, they are not ready to accept financial risk for something of which they have no control over the outcome. Building a traders' mentality is a must for trading success but this can take quite some time. Regrettably this is not an area where short cuts can be taken or a formula learnt. Traders quickly come to acknowledge that despite being familiar with winning strategies, systems and other techniques, successful trading is far more of a psychological dilemma. Ultimately, there will be virtually no chance to overcome the fear, confusion and despair that can be inherent in trading without a basic understanding of trading psychology.

Developing the trader's mindset or trading psychology is 'something' that a trader creates from existing personality traits that are not initially related to trading, but surface from trading without method understanding. Trading, with its inherent characteristic of accepting financial risk while participating in unknown outcomes, is certainly 'dangerous' and thus the more preparation and understanding there is, the better.

Trading is a performance related activity. Stress and mental pressures can be factors affecting the ability to function and to make profits. As trading differs from other businesses, it is especially helpful to note that success is not a function of how clever, smart or academically applied you are and the traditional working day of 9 to 5 doesn't apply in trading. What is of importance is attitude – attitude on how to deal with the daily grind of two steps forward and three steps back and how to deal with the predictable unfavourable situations that can and do occur in the markets. Slumps are inevitable for it is impossible to win 100 % of the time, especially as good trades don't always necessarily work out as most people react differently when they are under pressure. People have a tendency to be more emotional or reactive and will tense up, with judgement often becoming impaired.

28.1.2   The 'Game' of Trading

The common perception of foreign exchange trading is that it is some kind of game. Those involved are seen as players who are aggressively seeking risks, fighting to beat the market at large. The mantra is 'no reward without risk'. However, the harsh reality is that games are controlled by strict mathematical rules. The player loses – the bank always wins in the end. But if trading is really a game, how come not all of these players lose, after all banks are players too?

The answer is that there are different kinds of risk associated with different kinds of games. For example, roulette, where each spin of the wheel is a new game with each outcome being statistically independent from all preceding games. Just because the ball landed on black the last six times does not increase the probability that the next result will be red. On the other hand, blackjack is a different game, where analysis is key to beating the house. Roulette is a series of statistically independent events and outcomes cannot be forecast even with a perfect knowledge of the past. In blackjack the current hand is influenced by proceeding hands and analysis is possible. Clearly, foreign exchange prices are more like blackjack than roulette. The next movement in price is influenced by preceding moves.

For example, when an exchange rate moves, it has a direct impact on the psychology of the market. If the price moves up sharply, those that are 'short' may panic and buy-in, or if they are convinced that they are right and that the exchange rates are set to fall, they may even sell more. In addition, those who need to cover physical needs may also panic and buy. Those market participants who are 'long' (i.e. those that have bought ahead because they were speculating on a price rise) may sell to take profits, or may add to their existing positions. The reaction will depend very much on the overall make-up of the current exposure of the participants but it will most definitely be influenced by previous price movements. Additionally, a trader will also have to take into account the long-term and short-term trends in the exchange rates.

28.1.3   Rules

Successful traders will always acknowledge the importance of psychology in their trading, employing some if not all of the following:

- Discipline – like most things in life, without it you won't succeed. Discipline is sticking to the plan, including your stops and entry points. It is the hardest, but most important rule of all.

- Know your purpose – know why you are trading, whether if it is for the thrill or to make a living. Whatever it is, you will enjoy it more and trade better if you know why you are doing it.
- Trade only what you can afford to lose – trading is risky, don't fund trading with money, which if lost, could place financial difficulty on the institution or yourself.
- Maintain mental clarity – the ability to free oneself from concerns that might otherwise be distracting. Whether they be family, friends, markets or financial, always aim for a complete clarity of mind. Have clear goals and maintaining mental focus will help in sticking to the plan and assist in not making rash decisions based on emotion.
- Walk before running – learned knowledge and practical experience in the markets are the best teachers in the longer term. It is best to start with small amounts of contracts in less volatile markets and build from there.
- Don't place all your equity in any single position – one of the keys to success in trading is lasting in the game. Don't over commit to any one position.
- Accept that the market is always right – the market cannot be controlled by any one person alone and thus it has to be accepted that it will move regardless of what you want it to do. Fear, greed and hope can cloud one's vision of the market and can cause emotional responses detrimental to trading. Accept the fact that the market will go where it wants to go.
- Don't trade too many markets – professional traders tend to concentrate and focus on a few select markets and master them completely.
- Trade with definite goals in mind – profits belong to those who make decisions and act – not those who react. The trading plan should not only focus on the best time to get in but also when to get out. This involves setting a view for profit taking or loss minimization. It is better to set a stop for a loss amount and stick to it. If in profit, it is a good plan to set a stop to take a minimum profit whilst still giving the trade the potential for further profit.
- Stick to the plan – it is prudent to make minor adjustments throughout the trading period, but don't let the ups and downs of the market affect your overall game plan. Unless the market conditions that led to the placing of the trade change, don't abandon the original objective.
- Don't follow the crowd – when the newspaper calls a bull market, it is possibly time to sell. Most traders are uncomfortable when the position is popular with the public at large. However, the opposite may well be true if the 'crowd' is mostly made-up of institutional and hedge fund traders.
- Admit that you are wrong – don't fall in love with a losing position. If it is wrong, admit it, get out and wait for another opportunity.
- Let profits run until there is a reason to cash in – whether that is a trading signal, a fundamental factor or initial objective.
- Watch carefully for market divergence – professional traders are always on the lookout for market divergence. If the market sentiment is bearish but then breaks through technical resistance levels, it can often be a good indicator to buy.

- Over reactions – some of the best trades are the ones executed on over reactions, for example if the Dow Jones is down 150 points, the SPI may open 60 to 80 points down. In a number of situations this will be the low or close to the low of the day and a profitable buying opportunity can be the result. When the market presents an opportunity like this, be quick and decisive.
- Be careful when placing 'stop loss' orders – it is smart to use stops so that losses can be limited if the market moves against the position held. However, avoid setting them too close to the current price or on an obvious support or resistance levels.
- Picking highs and lows – this is not easy for anyone to do. Instead, it is better to ride the trend or movement for as long as possible and look to exit when it is showing signs of losing momentum.

28.1.4 Common Psychological Trading Issues

As mentioned above, trading can be stressful and if done every day, you can become tired and your judgement dulled. When that happens, you will begin to lose money. It makes sense to have a break every now and again and do something completely unrelated to trading. This can often give a new look at the markets and sharpen trading skills. Thus not only keep fresh but also keep healthy because trading activities blended with physical activity can help keep a clear mind. Trading is time consuming but provides the opportunity for growth, both financially and personally. It therefore makes sense to give yourself every chance to be successful by incorporating physical exercise into the trading day.

What's more, fear of failure, in one form or another, arises in all traders. The fear of admitting the trade is wrong, of being stopped out or of taking a loss, or the fear of position reversing and then feeling let down, or simply the fear to trade. In most of these examples, the trader's ego is at stake. Also, most traders crave the need for instant gratification, in other words needing instant approval from the markets for their trading actions.

In brief, the most common psychological barriers to successful trading include:

- Not defining a loss or not taking a profit or loss.
- Getting locked into a belief – the market is wrong and I am right, locking into self-belief and ignoring what the market is saying.
- 'Kamikaze' trading – trading just because you are angry or feel betrayed.
- Euphoric trading – feeling invincible or untouchable.
- Not catching a break-out or not focusing on opportunities.
- Not consistently applying a trading system.
- Not having a well defined money management system.
- Not being in the right state of mind.

In most cases, common psychological trading issues centre on the fact that for one reason or another, the trader is not following their chosen trading approach or system, preferring instead to wing it or trade on their emotions, which in trading will always end in trouble. The goal as a trader is to maintain an even keel, striving emotionally to maintain an even balance with regard to both wins and losses.

28.2   PSYCHOLOGY OF PRICE MOVEMENT

28.2.1   Some Insight Into Price Discovery

People new to trading often look at a price chart and wonder why the price is constantly oscillating or moving – doesn't it have a fixed price that can be determined? In answering this question, it is best to look at price discovery, which is the determination of a fair market value for any commodity. This is the process by which the buyers believe prices are rising and sellers believe prices are falling. The result is trading at an equilibrium price. Once buyers and sellers make their trades, their impact on the market dissolves until they exit their respective positions. As a result, there are two aspects to every trade – each will exit their position and other traders will react to their decision.

A trader's reaction to price movement affects the three participants in every market situation:

- The longs who want higher prices
- The shorts who are looking for lower prices.
- Traders on the sideline, who have not bought or sold. Clearly, the traders in this group have mixed views on market direction and wait for further indication before entering.

It should be noted that the market expectations of the longs and the shorts are exactly opposite and this group of traders has the greatest potential impact since they have not participated in the market to this point. As the market moves, so the market bias will change. A bullish trader may decide to go long on a 'break-out' above the current trading range conversely to a bearish trader looking to go short. These decisions by the 'sideliners' can have adverse effects on traders who already hold a position in the market. Plus, during a period of consolidation (narrow trading range) the longs (traders that have bought) and the shorts (traders that have sold) are sensitive to the first trade outside of this range. As price moves higher or lower one group is increasing profit while the other group has increasing loss.

28.3   BASIC PRICE MOVEMENT PATTERN

Figure 28.1 is an example of a typical price movement pattern. The patterns can be explained thus:

- Sideways price movement between points A and B – from this consolidation period, an advance in the price develops into a bull market.

Price

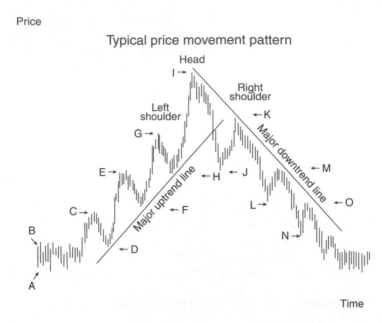

Figure 28.1   Typical price movement pattern

- When the market advances to point C – since the trading range was long and narrow the buy orders above the market could be quite numerous (buy on the break of the range). When the market advances past point B, buy orders start entering the market. These buy orders can be one of three types: adding to a long position, covering a previous short position, or initiating a long position. At point C previous longs are satisfied and profit-taking begins and the market dips to point D.

This price movement demonstrates a distinct psychological attitude. The net effect of the rally from A to C would be the beginning of a psychological change in all three groups. The result of the change would be a different tone to the market, where support (buyers) could be expected from all three groups on dips. This price pattern occurs until we reach point I, where the downturn begins and the picture changes.

- As the market begins to advance from point J to point K, traders with previously established long positions are taking profits by selling out. Most of the hard-nosed traders with short positions have previously covered their short positions adding no significant new buying impetus to the market. In fact, having witnessed the recent decline, they may be adding to their short positions ('averaging' and some might call it 'suicide').
- If the rally toward the contract high fails (point J to K), it signals that the bull market has indeed run its course and will not continue. If the open interest also declines during the rally from J to K, it is another sign that it was not new buying that caused the rally but short covering.

- As profit-taking and new short-selling forces the market to decline from point K, the next critical point is the reactionary low point at J. A major failure or bear signal is flashed if the market penetrates this prominent low following an abortive attempt to establish new contract highs.

In the language of chartists, a head-and-shoulders reversal pattern has been completed. But rather than simply explaining away price patterns with names, it is important to understand the psychology of the market at these different points. It is also important to explain why certain price levels are significant. In a bear market, the attitudes of the traders would be reversed. Each decline would find the bears more confident and prosperous and the bulls more depressed and threadbare. With the psychology diametrically opposite, the pattern completely reverses itself to form a series of lower highs and lower lows. At some point (the end of a downtrend) the bears would be unwilling to add to their previously established short positions. Those who were already long the market and had refused to sell out. Traders not in the market who were perhaps attempting unsuccessfully to short the market at higher levels will begin to find the long side of the market more attractive. The first rally that 'carries too high to be bearish' would signal another possible trend reversal.

In a broad sense, it should appear as an upward series of waves of successively higher highs and higher lows. This process continues until the first signal that a reversal in psychology is beginning to overtake the market. It demonstrates a noticeable lack of support on a dip that carries too far to be bullish. For example, the decline from point I to point J would be the classic example of a dip that carried too far. Recognizing that the market may be in the process of 'topping out' they are prepared to sell the next rally. The earliest indication of a change in market psychology to one with bearish overtones may be an advance (from H to I) that is greater than the other previous advances. Now the picture has changed. The whole process begins to unwind and the process by which the market advanced now declines.

28.4   SUMMARY

With this basic understanding of market psychology through the three phases of a market, a trader is better equipped to appreciate the significance of all technical price patterns. No one expects to establish long positions at the low, but development of a feel for market psychology is the beginning of the search for trades that only hindsight could improve on. Furthermore, the effect our emotions have on price movement can be seen in the changing psychology of the market; fear, greed and frustration all manifest themselves in a patterned movement.

CONCLUDING REMARKS

The accessibility of screen based trading has transformed the markets. Today, many novice traders believe that all they have to do is sit down in front of a computer and begin trading, but they could not be further from the truth. Critical decisions have to be made, like what type of trader you want to be (day-trader or position trader), your psychological makeup, comfort and support levels, trading strategy, the markets you are most interested in, technology requirements and your trading goals. These all create a sound foundation, but this is not the end of the story.

At the end of the day, consistency is far more important than brilliance. It may take years to develop both the 'science' of trading which represents your trading skills and the 'art' of trading which represents judgement and mindset. Most new traders fail here because they don't have the discipline to work on their trading approach until it is profitable. While it is important to be focused on trading, there is a line at which focus can become obsession, but do not cross this line.

The key to achieving mental mastery over trading is believing that you can actually do it. Everyone is capable of being a successful trader if they truly believe they can be. Believe in the power of belief.

29
Final Remarks

On the foreign exchange markets, major currencies are traded like commodities. Although there is no centralized exchange, individuals are linked to one another through sophisticated communications and information systems. Trading occurs in the prominent financial centres of the world, so that a foreign exchange market is active somewhere in the world every minute of the day. Hence it is a decentralized marketplace. The main players are corporations, individuals, major banks and central banks.

Participants transact in foreign currency not only for immediate delivery (**spot transactions**) but also for settlement at specific times in the future (**forward transactions**). The market participants on the other side of any trade must either have exactly opposite needs or be willing to take a speculative position. Typical transactions in the bank market range from $ 5 million to $ 50 million plus, although banks will handle smaller sizes but generally at slightly less favourable prices.

Besides the spot and forward markets, over the years, other markets have been developed that are gaining acceptance. **Foreign currency futures** contracts, which provide an alternative to the forward market, have been designed for a few major currencies. The advantages of these contracts are smaller contract size and the high degree of liquidity for small transactions. The disadvantages include the inflexibility of both standardized contract sizes and maturities and the higher costs on large transactions. **Options** on both currency futures and spot currency are also available and are growing in stature every day. **Foreign currency swaps** form another instrument that is used to provide long-dated forward cover of foreign currency exposure, especially against the flow of foreign currency debt.

Participants in the foreign exchange market need to keep abreast of their **fundamental** knowledge as well as learn how to use basic **technical** tools. Currency prices often reflect the underlying strength or weakness of the country's economy. For example, the strength of the dollar reflected the boom of the American economy over the past decade. If American economic growth is declining or is expected to decline, the expected return on American assets will fall, and the dollar may be pressured relative to other currencies. Also, a knowledge of **macroeconomic fundamentals** is critical for trading any currency. For example, Japan has suffered a no-growth economy for years and its nominal interest rates have hovered near zero percent. A trader needs to know that a strong Japanese yen is not a solution to these problems. Thus, in periods where the yen strengthens, traders should be wary of an official policy response to drive the yen lower. Hence, if a currency is very strong, the trader needs to know who is hurt and who is helped by that condition. A strong yen hurts the Japanese exporter who has to sell to America, but it helps the American carmakers in competition with Japanese exports.

Also, any currency trader needs to develop a **global perspective** and a feel for intermarket relationships. Interest rate trends are the most important external information source. If the American Federal Reserve cuts rates, the dollar should weaken. However, if the European Central Bank is expected to follow suit, interest rate trends will converge and the value of the currency may not change at all. A trader will need to follow not only the Chairman of the Federal Reserve, but also his counterparts in the European Central Bank and the Bank of Japan.

Currencies tend to be trendier than either stocks or commodities, and it is important to understand the trend from both a fundamental and a technical point of view. Currencies cannot reverse trends very easily because economies do not reverse quickly relative to one another. However, a successful trader will recognize how fundamentals and technicals combine to indicate a trend reversal. Of course, finding the trend reversal before it happens is the 'Holy Grail' of trading. No one can be expected to be successful all the time.

29.1   AND WHAT OF THE FUTURE?

The foreign exchange trading market is changing dramatically, especially with the arrival of **electronic trading**. Today's electronic environment means that participants are looking for faster and tighter pricing with faster relevant news flows than ever before. Also, market participants are looking for trading platforms, which are Internet enabled, scalable across regions, reliable and safeguarded against crashes, and which can be integrated with various risk management systems. The future lies largely in the ability of market makers to deliver a better service to their clients, whether it is offering transaction, deal capture, trade history facilities or risk management capabilities. At the end of the day, it is all about the value chain and how it is delivered to clients. Internet trading might be here to stay, but the foreign exchange market should not expect volumes to increase significantly. At the end of the day, the foreign exchange market will always be a people-to-people marketplace.

In addition, there is a new 'aspect' to foreign exchange trading which has entered the market over the last couple of years and needs to be taken seriously for the future – namely **systematic trading** and **algorithmic trading**. Both areas are of growing importance among financial institutions and can certainly not be ignored in the future.

So, in conclusion, foreign exchange is both a science and an art. Risk can be quantified and alternatives identified to reduce or eliminate it. But judgement, personal attitudes towards risk, as well as other personal and corporate orientations, are required for consistent position management. I repeat again, profit opportunities and potential loss *are equal and opposite*.

Index

Index compiled by Annette Musker